'A riveting, comforting and much-nee
when so many are struggling.'
Debby Wright, national director, Vineyar

CU91507860

'This book is just like its author – cc
Though church leadership can ind
thousand cuts, with great vulnerabiliç
weaves together the genuine pain of personal testimony with the very
real promises of God's Word to offer renewed hope and conviction to
those serving within the trenches of Christian ministry. Thoroughly
recommended!'
*Danny Murphy, AOG national leadership team, lead pastor of Life Church
Europe*

'I recently heard a presentation about trust and leadership. The formula
given was transparency + consistency + empathy = trust. Howard
displays all three of these qualities within the pages of this book. He
consistently returns to the Scriptures; his transparency, which includes
his own battles, is commendable; and his empathy towards fellow
wounded Christ-followers comes through time and again. There are
some books you wish you'd read before you went through "stuff". This
is one of them. Highly recommended for leaders and followers alike.'
*Steve Campbell, national director of the Global Leadership Network UKI,
senior pastor at The C3 Church, Cambridge*

'The book very sensitively handles the significant area of
discouragement and disappointment that every Christian will meet on
their faith journey at some time or another. In a clearly thought out and
practical way, the book illustrates how it is possible to turn to God and
find comfort in those times of deep doubt and suffering. Having the
freedom to pour out all our negative experiences and deepest emotions,
and to experience God in a new way coming alongside us, enables and
encourages us to hold on to hope and faith in a good God who loves us
and is for us. This is such an important message for the times we live
in, and it is embodied in this gem of a book.'
*Sue and Andy Glover, Fresh Streams national network leaders, Hoole Baptist
Church leaders*

'*Hold on to Hope* is a profound and compassionate guide for those facing discouragement. Drawing from candid personal experiences and rich biblical insights, Howard, alongside contributions from inspirational leaders like Katia Adams, Andy Kind and Dr R T Kendall, provides practical wisdom and timely encouragement to learn how to process and walk through discouragement from multiple angles and in varying ways. Because of that, this book offers a lifeline of hope, making it an essential read for anyone seeking comfort and strength in challenging times. Highly recommended.'
Simon Holley, Newfrontiers, Catalyst family of churches leader; senior pastor, King's Arms Church, Bedford; founder of www.therawleader.com

'Howard has a very natural writing style that draws the reader into the heart of the message. *Hold on to Hope* is full of truths that make you pause and ask honest questions. It is written with a humility and faith that gives the reader hope even when things seem difficult. I recommend it highly, knowing it will bless your soul.'
Harold Afflu, senior minister, City Gates, Ilford, member of Elim national leadership team

'With honesty and profound Bible insights, Howard and his friends help us to see that there are good reasons to feel battle weary, that we have permission to feel and to weep and to bring our pain and discouragement to God. This book is relevant for every believer, and I am certain I will come back to it again.'
Tom Scrivens, Newfrontiers, relational mission church community group leader, lead pastor, Hope Church, Ipswich

'As an author, book coach and publisher, I deeply appreciate this book and its author who, like me, has the gift of dyslexia. If you want encouragement, I recommend reading this book.'
Matt Bird, CEO of PublishU

'Howard has written a well-researched and timely book for those who feel discouraged. *Hold on to Hope* balances hard-hitting facts with compassion, and depth with humour; a great companion to those who need a dose of hope.'
Lauren Windle, journalist, author and presenter

'Howard's book *Hold on to Hope* is well researched, thoroughly biblical and easy to read. It is written from his heart and is an honest account of his personal experience of the debilitating pain of discouragement and the way the Lord led him into freedom, which is the rightful inheritance of every child of God. Read it and be encouraged!'
John Noble, chair of the UK National Charismatic and Pentecostal Leaders Conference 1984-2006

'*Hold on to Hope* is a remarkable, insight-laden, question-asking, reflection-generating book from a man who honestly voices something of his own journey and travail to help others. From the introductory poem to the helpful and provocative chapter questions, this is a book for everyone. It is for everyone at some stage in their lives to find affinity with the challenge of discouragement described. I highly recommend this book for personal reflection and for better equipping us to walk with and encourage each other in ways that exhibit more understanding, compassion and empathy, yet also help us journey through discouragement to the beauty and strength beyond. Discouragement need not be the last word.'
Phil Norris, Basingstoke Community Churches leader, Forge Sphere leader

'This book is so good! I know it will be a huge blessing and encouragement to many other leaders who think they are the only ones struggling.'
Andy Worthington, head of church relations, Open Doors UK & Ireland

'This book authentically captures our human frailty and the power of finding even small strands of hope to hold on to. Disappointment, loss, anxiety and being let down by others can all lead to a debilitating sense of hopelessness. With honest reflections from a variety of contributors and drawing on the profound wisdom of the Bible, this book will not only encourage you, but also make space for you to ponder where you're at and lead you to an understanding of how you can re-engage with a sense of hope.'
Ellie Gage, CEO Kintsugi Hope

'Having known Howard for some time now, and enjoyed his anointed ministry, particularly at Westminster Chapel, I was initially surprised to discover that discouragement could touch him. As someone who has

poured his life into others and preached the good news of God to many people, I always saw Howard as one of those set apart for a special purpose in the kingdom of God and, therefore, in some way, immune from discouragement. This book on hope and the honesty with which he writes about suffering and, at times, crippling discouragement is not only refreshingly brave but also incredibly liberating. Brilliantly paced, with heartfelt illustrations, interviews and real-life glimpses of grace, this book is thoroughly biblical, encouraging, real and filled with hope throughout. I have no doubt that this work from Howard will be a source of help for many people to become strong in the broken places.'
William Wade, former British soldier, Baptist minister and author

'I intend to hold on to this book. Spoiler alert: Let me pick out a few gems. Written in a disarmingly winsome and vulnerable way, you will explore the disappointment of delay, how to talk to yourself rather than listen to yourself, and how to turn irritation into invitation by growing your knowledge of who you are in Christ. Encouragement is a gift of the Spirit, and this book is the gift that just keeps on giving, silencing the echo chambers of discouragement and screaming hope! I encourage you to read and hold on to it.'
Dr Andy Hutchinson, global mission director of Christian Explored

'This is a refreshingly honest, thoughtful and captivating book. Howard has delightfully captured what it means to have the unconditionally loving arms of the Father surround us, even in the darkest times.'
Tim Grainger, head of Employment Law and partner at Fiona Bruce Solicitors, Warrington, a leading Christian law firm

HOLD ON TO HOPE

How to navigate discouragement in everyday life

Howard Satterthwaite

with life-giving wisdom from conversations with Paul and
Becky Harcourt, Katia Adams, Andy Kind, Esha*,
Rachael Newham, Tola Doll Fisher
and Dr R T Kendall

instant
apostle

First published in Great Britain in 2025

Instant Apostle
104A The Drive
Rickmansworth
Herts
WD3 4DU

Copyright © Howard Satterthwaite 2025

The author has asserted his rights under Section 77 of the Copyright, Designs and Patents Act, 1988, to be identified as the author of the work.

All rights reserved. No portion of this book may be reproduced or transmitted in any form or by any means, electronic or mechanical, including photocopying and recording, or by any information storage and retrieval system, without permission in writing from the publisher.

Unless otherwise indicated, all Scripture quotations are taken from the Holy Bible, New International Version® Anglicised, NIV® Copyright © 1979, 1984, 2011 by Biblica, Inc.® Used by permission. All rights reserved worldwide.

Scripture quotations marked 'ESV' are from the ESV® Bible (The Holy Bible, English Standard Version®), copyright © 2001 by Crossway, a publishing ministry of Good News Publishers. Used by permission. All rights reserved.

Scripture quotations marked 'AMP' are taken from the Amplified® Bible (AMP). Copyright © 2015 by The Lockman Foundation. Used by permission. www.Lockman.org.

Every effort has been made to seek permission to use copyright material reproduced in this book. The publisher apologises for those cases where permission might not have been sought and, if notified, will formally seek permission at the earliest opportunity.

The views and opinions expressed in this work are those of the author and do not necessarily reflect the views and opinions of the publisher.

British Library Cataloguing-in-Publication Data

A catalogue record for this book is available from the British Library.

This book and all other Instant Apostle books are available from Instant Apostle:

Website: www.instantapostle.com

Email: info@instantapostle.com

ISBN 978-1-912726-92-9

Printed in Great Britain.

To my wonderful wife, Holly – thank you so much for helping me to hold on to hope through my many discouragements.

Contents

Author's note 13

Foreword: Cathy Madavan 15

Introduction.. 19

1. Trust again: Paul and Becky Harcourt.......................... 33

2. Why, my soul, are you downcast? 41

3. Try tears: Katia Adams 55

4. Where is your hope?... 63

5. Pursue purpose: Andy Kind 77

6. What have you forgotten? 83

7. Godly faith over ungodly fear: Esha* 95

8. To what extent are you enquiring? 99

9. Begin with beloved: Rachael Newham 107

10. How are your neighbours? 115

11. Sanctify success: Tola Doll Fisher 123

12. Is there enough grace in your gait? 131

13. Forgive freely: Dr R T Kendall 137

14. Where are you? 143

15. Conclusion 145

Kintsugi Hope: Journeying towards wholeness 150

Open Doors UK & Ireland: Standing with the persecuted Church 152

Acknowledgements 155

Author's note

100% of the author's income will be donated equally between Kintsugi Hope (Charity No. 1175529) and Open Doors UK & Ireland (Charity No. 1125684).

The full content of this book does not necessarily reflect the beliefs and opinions of the contributors or organisations supported by sales of the book.

Foreword

You are not alone. These are perhaps four of the most powerful and hope-filled words in the English language, and words we often need to hear. To put it another way – life, relationships and leadership can be challenging (an understatement), and we may certainly feel alone sometimes. But there is hope. You are not the only person to experience life's curveballs or to face discouragement. Of course, the specifics of your story may be unique and not everybody's offloading of their own experience 'just like yours' will be helpful. But we all know that isolation, secret self-scrutiny and comparison with others whom we perceive to not be struggling are in fact highways towards destructive thinking and further isolation.

That's why reflecting upon Scripture and other people's lived experience can be so helpful and liberating. Where another person has experienced a similar dilemma, diagnosis or life experience, we can benefit and draw strength from their testimony. It's why conferences, forums, gatherings and friendships are often so valuable. Together we gain wisdom, insight and strategies. But most of all, we gain hope.

Like many others, my husband and I have navigated plenty of challenges over the years, including disability, grief, church leadership issues, family crises and painful relationship breakdown. But isn't it always the case – life is lived in the tension between battles and blessings? Rick Warren, pastor of Saddleback Church for many years and author of *The Purpose Driven Life*, once described blessings and battles as akin to train tracks, we simultaneously navigate and live between.[1] It is completely normal. Somehow, we learn to travel along those tracks – sometimes effortlessly, sometimes cautiously, and sometimes painfully and slowly. Thankfully, that journey is a hundred times more sustainable and hopeful when we travel with God and with others.

This is why this book is so important. Alongside the hugely encouraging and helpful biblical input, Howard has invited others into a timely, transparent and innately theological conversation about hope. Each contributor has (with some vulnerability) pulled back the curtain and revealed something significant about their life. As you read their story and glean from their hard-earned wisdom, you may well find yourself nodding and acknowledging their experience as one you resonate with. But more than that, you are invited into this conversation. As you turn the pages, rather than being a mere witness to the experience of others, you are given the opportunity to be an active participant in the dialogue. Where there are questions that invite honest and reflective learning, you will no doubt be encouraged and strengthened by the time given to respond.

---

[1] Rick Warren, interview with *Decision Magazine*, 'Preparing for Eternity on Purpose', 22nd October 2004, www.decisionmagazine.com/preparing-for-eternity-on-purpose (accessed 12th February 2025).

So, as a leader, as a disciple of Jesus, or simply as a person navigating the twin tracks of battles and blessings, I believe you will be reminded repeatedly in this book that there is indeed hope. Others have travelled before you and are also standing with you now. God is for you and with you. And, crucially, whatever opportunities or challenges you may face in the coming days, this book will remind you that you are never alone – which truly is a hope to hold on to. I thoroughly recommend it.

Cathy Madavan, speaker, writer, broadcaster
www.cathymadavan.com
January 2025

Introduction

This poem appeared in the Christian newspaper *Evangelicals Now* in October 2022:[2]

I am a pastor, not a punchbag for your pain.
Or had you forgotten that I am human too?
I can see it can help to have someone to blame,
but is this actually about me or more about you?

Your mumblings became grumblings when life
became harder.
I'm so sorry – it really does hurt me to see you
suffer.
Truly, I seek your best, even though you always
know 'better';
I want you to rest in the embrace of the World's
Greatest Lover.

You say my preaching lacks depth and isn't
exegetical;
others tell me it's too rich and rigidly Scriptural.

---

[2] Used with the kind permission of *Evangelicals Now*, e-n.org.uk/your-views/2022-11-a-heartfelt-plea-from-an-anonymous-pastor (accessed 12th February 2025).

You say I'm detached, distant and even
disinterested;
others tell me I'm inappropriately, emotionally
over-invested.

There are moments when I'm very tempted to
quit.
Did you know that? I expect not; perhaps you'd be
happier if I did.
I was actually signed off work with depression by
my GP.
But I didn't dare take it, fearing more criticism
against me.

I soldier on (calling not done) to be a good pastor,
only to fail and inevitably falter;
for only God can be worshipped at this altar –
that you desire me to die on for you.
Do you know that I am not your Saviour?

I write in support of unfairly treated pastors,
Yes, some have been abusive and done much
wrong,
but others are victims of proud church members;
wounded by the very community to which they
also belong.

Selah.[3]

Pastor Anon

---

[3] Meaning, despite the admitted absence of biblical certainty,
pause and reflect, which is one of the tools we'll try to employ
more positively together.

Look beyond the poor poetry to the pain that lies beneath. How can I say that? Because, yes, you guessed it, I wrote it. Is it one-sided? Yes. Am I also guilty of wrongdoing? Of course. But have I been beaten up by discouragement (despite being generously loved by many good church people)? Most certainly, yes.

A few years ago, my parents shared an intriguing story they'd heard about a former pastor of theirs. During one Sunday sermon, they abruptly halted their message, appearing agitated and angry. They then ran out of the building and were later kept in hospital under the Mental Health Act. At the time, I sympathised with the difficult situation they faced while arrogantly thinking, 'I'll never let that happen to me.' I was wrong.

According to Christian research giants Barna, 42 per cent of pastors thought about quitting the ministry in the year leading up to March 2022 – a significant increase on previous years, probably brought on by the global pandemic.[4] I wonder how much discouragement is to blame. Blocked goals. Broken dreams. Hopes deferred, making hearts sick.[5]

Fast forward with me to March 2023. I am emotionally and physically exhausted. I have decided to resign from my lead pastor role. How did this happen? In short, a relentless foe invaded my spirit – discouragement. It seized me with such force that it transformed into

---

[4] Barna Group, 'Pastors Share Top Reasons They've Considered Quitting Ministry in the Past Year', www.barna.com/research/pastors-quitting-ministry (accessed 8th January 2025).
[5] Proverbs 13:12.

debilitating depression, occasionally tightening into the stranglehold of despair. I found myself gasping for air, suffocating beneath the burden of seemingly unattainable expectations, both externally and internally imposed.

But because of the grace of God, I didn't give up, and neither should you. Aware of so many other sufferers, I felt stirred to read as much as I could, speak with as many people as possible and share what was helpful. This is the record of that experiment, turning these conversations into the edited contributor chapters featured in this book. Reflecting upon it now, having completed the initial draft, I can confidently affirm that 'victory is won through many advisors' (Proverbs 11:14). The Scriptures hold profound wisdom, and our triune God – Father, Son and Holy Spirit – genuinely desires for you to rediscover hope and embrace courage once more.

Within the pages of this book lies a potent elixir for weary souls – an antidote crafted to liberate us from the shackles of toxic discouragement. Its purpose is to protect us from the dangerous downward progression of disappointments taking us into the gruelling grip of discouragement, which could lead to depression. However, to truly harness the full transformative power of its contents, you'll need to make time to do its suggested action steps, engaging in a healthy amount of self-reflection, with the first question being, 'How does discouragement get at you?'

But if you're anything like me, you'll find it hard to slow down enough to do that. Yet you must. Like shaken jars of river water, we need to be still and let the sediment – the inner angst and everything else around – settle so we can see and think clearly. Please don't make the same mistake as I did. Instead, pause, breathe deeply, seek to be still for a few moments, and make space for our Divine Physician to do what He does best.

Discouragement comes at me in many ways, but 'you're not good enough' is the most common. It breaks down into: 'You're not knowledgeable enough,' 'You're not experienced enough,' and, 'You're not outgoing enough' (ie, too introverted).

Pause!
So how does discouragement get at you?
Take time to reflect on this for a few minutes.

According to Google, discouragement is 'a loss of confidence or enthusiasm; dispiritedness'.[6] The Latin prefix 'dis' means apart, so to be discouraged is to be separated from courage. Other dictionaries describe it as a loss of the inner resolve – both mentally and morally – to take risks and persevere in the face of difficulty. But it's more personal than that. The root of the word courage is 'cor' – the Latin word for heart. Discouragement invades the very core of our being.

The word 'discourage' or 'discouraged' appears six times in the ESV Bible translation.[7] The first occurrences in Numbers 32:7, 9 highlight its effect not just on a person's heart but the heart of a people. It takes away our confidence to take possession of what God has given. Isn't discouragement a loss of confidence in who we are in

---

[6] Google Dictionary, s.v. 'discouragement', tinyurl.com/y86ntr2d (accessed 8th January 2025).
[7] Numbers 32:7, 9; 2 Samuel 17:2; Ezra 4:4; Isaiah 42:4; Colossians 3:21.

Christ due to His victory at the cross – not savouring all the victory spoils of our salvation? The other references are connected with being weary, afraid, faint-hearted and quickly thrown into a state of panic.

Good company

As we embark on this journey together, it's good to know that we're not alone – and it's not just the two of us. The founder and former international director of Operation Mobilisation, George Verwer, wrote, 'Simple, straightforward discouragement is the biggest drain on our spiritual resources. No one is free of it; many suffer from it acutely.'[8]

Everyone with a beating heart battles discouragement, no matter how cool, calm and collected they pretend to be. Nineteenth-century preaching legend Charles Spurgeon and twenty-first-century creative writing genius J K Rowling experienced significant discouragement. Such people are helpful company in unhappy times, which is why this book is broken up by stories of faithful Christ-followers sharing their encouraging insights. They're supported by testimonies from our persecuted family around the world. Collectively, they've breathed catalytic oxygen into the burnt-out embers of my heart; I pray they'll greatly bless you, too.

It's also vital we recall revered characters of biblical history – Moses, Elijah, Job and Jonah – all of whom

---

[8] George Verwer, *No Turning Back*, Waynesboro, GA: Operation Mobilisation Literature Ministry, 1983, p 101, ia801005.us.archive.org/16/items/noturningback_201908/No%20Turning%20Back.pdf (accessed 3rd January 2025).

became so discouraged they wished for death. Overwhelmed by the weighty responsibilities of leadership, Moses cried out to God, 'If this is how you are going to treat me, please go ahead and kill me' (Numbers 11:15). Exhausted from intense ministry and intimidating threats, Elijah exclaimed, 'I have had enough, LORD ... Take my life; I am no better than my ancestors' (1 Kings 19:4).

Interestingly, it was these two spiritual giants who stood beside Jesus at His transfiguration.[9] Super saints but also broken believers. But why them? In addition to representing the Law and the Prophets, could it be they were comforting Christ (in His humanity) with the comfort they'd received?[10] Were they helping to prepare Him to face deep discouragement in the Garden of Gethsemane and fearful forsakenness on the cross? Did their greatest ministry, then, come not from their strengths but from their weaknesses?

Kintsugi

My wife took me to a kintsugi workshop in London for my forty-fourth birthday. If you've not heard of kintsugi, it's a Japanese word that means 'gold joining'. It's been called 'the poetic mend' – making a broken object new and much more precious by filling its cracks with gold. Artist, researcher and former editor of *Ceramic Review*, Bonnie Kemske, described it like this: 'an intimate metaphoric

---

[9] Matthew 17:1-9.
[10] 2 Corinthians 1:4.

narrative of loss and recovery, breakage and restoration, tragedy and the ability to overcome it'.[11]

What if *your* brokenness could be made beautiful? What if discouragement is designed to make you stronger – as the wind to the roots of a tree?

During the workshop, we each chose a plate or bowl to break using a hammer. What struck me as intriguing was the need for skill, training and careful supervision to ensure that the ceramic vessel didn't splinter or shatter into pieces. This raises a fascinating parallel: could this be an illustration of how the sovereignty of God operates in our lives through moments of hardship and adversity? 'We are hard pressed on every side, but not crushed; perplexed, but not in despair; persecuted, but not abandoned; struck down, but not destroyed' (2 Corinthians 4:8-9).

Whereas breaking took seconds, repairing each crack with glue and imitation gold dust took fifteen minutes – more than an hour for the complete restoration. This is the expedited budget version: traditional kintsugi restoration can take two to three months! Isn't that how life often works?

As I've reflected on this imbalance between breaking and healing, my thinking is that God permits it so we can spend more time in the arms of the Divine Physician.

---

[11] Bonnie Kemske, *Kintsugi: The Poetic Mend*, London: Herbert Press, 2021, p 12.

Pause!

Where in your life have you experienced a sudden 'break' that required a much longer season of healing? How might viewing that slower restoration as time spent in the arms of the Divine Physician transform your perspective on what you're going through?

Strength in weakness

The Prince of Preachers, Charles Spurgeon, mentioned above, suffered depression – an anguish his wife, Susannah, described as 'deep and violent'.[12] But this thorn in the flesh[13] gave unexpected power to his ministry. One Sunday, he preached on Matthew 27:46, 'My God, my God, why have you forsaken me?' – speaking from his own experiences without saying so. 'I heard my own chains clank,' he said, 'while I tried to preach to my fellow-prisoners in the dark, but I could not tell why I was brought into such an awful horror of darkness, for which I condemned myself.'[14]

The next day, a man bearing the marks of despair came to see him. He said:

'I never before, in my life, heard any man speak who seemed to know my heart. Mine is a terrible case,

---

[12] Charles Ray, 'The Life of Susannah Spurgeon', in *Morning Devotions by Susannah Spurgeon: Free Grace and Dying Love*, Edinburgh: Banner of Truth, 2006, p 166.

[13] 2 Corinthians 12:7.

[14] Charles Spurgeon, *An All-Round Ministry: A Selection from his Presidential Addresses at the Annual Conferences of the Pastors College*, 1900, eBook, www.monergism.com/all-around-ministry-ebook (accessed 29th November 2024), pp 173-74.

but on Sunday morning, you painted me to the life and preached as if you had been inside my soul.' By God's grace, I saved that man from suicide, and led him into the gospel's light and liberty, but I know I could not have done it if I had not myself been confined in the dungeon in which he lay.[15]

Disappointment, discouragement, depression and despair should not be seen as disqualifying disorders. Nope, it's the opposite. Our shared experiences of them, in union with Christ, equip and qualify us for effective ministry. Weakness should not be viewed as failure, because it's the foundation for strength.

Questions

You may have noticed that you've encountered several questions already in this book. I've taken this approach because I really value them. As a junior courtroom lawyer specialising in criminal law, I was trained to ask them; they are, after all, fundamental tools of the profession. I've also experienced their transformative power as a senior practitioner coach.

In the pages of Scripture, we see God using them to rescue us from the muddy mires into which we can sink. Consider His first, to Adam and Eve after their disobedience. When they were consumed by fear and shame, our *all-knowing* God asked, 'Where are you?' (Genesis 3:9). It was a catalyst for reorientation, an invitation to come out from hiding and enjoy God's nurturing presence, a call to confront challenging realities

---

[15] Spurgeon, *An All-Round Ministry*, pp 173-174.

with the strength bestowed by heaven. And it's like Father, like Son: in *Twenty Questions Jesus Asked*, former Bishop of Oxford John Pritchard wrote, 'Jesus was brilliant at asking the right questions, the sort that opened up new spiritual space and helped people to listen to whispers and hopes from deep within themselves.'[16]

Questions also serve as a tool for slowing down our hurried pace of life. We often lack the discipline of self-reflection, getting caught up in the perpetual rat race – charging around to keep everyone happy. Not long ago, I got caught speeding and had to take the National Speed Awareness Course. I'm actually glad I did – it was a real eye-opener. The science they shared was challenging: driving faster doesn't actually save you much time, if any, but it seriously increases the risk of accidents happening. Just one mile an hour over the limit can make stopping distances way longer than we think.

That hit me on a deeper level, too. Life's the same – we're always rushing, but at what cost? We can go through life at a million miles an hour, forgetting, as one of the most influential Asian theologians, Kosuke Koyama, reminds us, that we serve a three-mile-an-hour God.[17] That's walking pace, by the way. This is the deliberate speed God chose to come alongside us – a gentle reminder for us to embrace a slower, more loving way of living that has time for God, ourselves and others.

---

[16] John Pritchard, *Twenty Questions Jesus Asked: And How They Speak To Us Today*, London: SPCK, 2022, pp x–xi.
[17] Kosuke Koyama, *Three Mile an Hour God*, London: SCM Press, 2021.

This book, therefore, is designed a little differently from some. Its backbone is seven restorative questions intended to anchor us to hope (again). These chapters are broken up with pause points and conclude with stop-and-think sections to help us slow down, to reflect on what's been shared and to encounter God.

David

When grappling with discouragement, a verse that has always captivated my attention is 1 Samuel 30:6. David returned from avoiding fighting for the Philistines against his own people to discover the Amalekites had pillaged his Ziklag homestead. The devastation was overwhelming, with the entire settlement burned to the ground and their loved ones taken captive. David and his men were overcome with grief and 'wept aloud' (v 4). Amid this dire situation, however, and despite David's outraged men talking of stoning him, we find these words: 'But David found strength in the LORD his God' (v 6). In the Amplified version the phrase is 'felt strengthened and encouraged'. According to Strong's Concise Dictionary, the Hebrew word being translated here can mean:

> 2388. חָזַק châzaq, khaw-zak´; a prim. root; to fasten upon; hence to seize, be strong ... be of good (take) courage (-ous, -ly), encourage (self), be established, fasten, force, fortify, make hard, harden, help, (lay) hold (fast), lean, maintain, play the man, mend, become (wax) mighty, prevail, be recovered, repair, retain, seize, be (wax) sore, strengthen (self), be stout, be (make, shew, wax) strong (-er), be sure,

take (hold), be urgent, behave self valiantly, withstand.[18]

I particularly like the idea of David fastening himself upon and cleaving to the Lord his God. The sense of him repairing himself in the Lord is also intriguing. What word(s) caught your attention?

The big question, though, is, 'How?' Right? *How* did David encourage himself in the Lord?

The essence of this book lies in our collective endeavour – mine and others', and yours – to address this transformational question. We'll answer it together by delving into the life of David, drawing insights from Scripture and sharing personal experiences. David serves as an immensely inspirational figure to explore. He grants us permission to feel and weep just as Jesus did, and to pray our pain to God, as exemplified in Psalm 38. David experienced deep discouragement stemming from his own sins, as well as injustices inflicted upon him. Remarkably, he's called 'a man after [God's] own heart' (1 Samuel 13:14). There's so much wisdom for us to glean from his life.

---

[18] James Strong, *A Concise Dictionary of the Words in the Greek Testament and the Hebrew Bible*, vol 2, Bellingham, WA: Logos Bible Software, 2009, p 38.

Stop and think

- Discouragement poisons our hearts from living courageously for God's good purposes. Where have external pressures, like criticism, people-pleasing and perfectionism, distanced you from your identity and calling in Christ?

- In moments when you feel like a damaged vessel, how might your brokenness be an invitation to experience more of the gold of God's goodness? In other words, where could 'kintsugi' happen in your life?

1
Trust again
Paul and Becky Harcourt

Paul and Becky have been leading All Saints' Woodford Wells in London since 1995. Paul previously served as the national leader of the New Wine network, and Becky spent seven years on its national leadership team. Together, they're actively involved in leadership development and frequently speak at conferences across the UK and Europe. They've also authored two highly regarded books: Growing in Circles *and* Walking on Water *(Northampton: River Publishing & Media Ltd, 2016/2017). For more information, visit www.asww.org.uk*

Repeated setbacks and thwarted expectations

Discouragement comes when things keep not working out and our hopes are continually set back. When we're in its grip, it's hard even to be encouraged by the good things happening. It robs us of joy and energy, making it difficult to dream and imagine something could be different.

For Becky and me, the challenges we've faced include thwarted expectations of what parenthood would look like.

Both our children are on the autistic spectrum, with our eldest being low-functioning autistic, non-verbal and in many ways stuck at a toddler level of development. Now, in his mid-twenties, he has moved into supported living, but prior to this we spent years caring for him, which significantly impacted our home life and energy levels.

Temperament and tragedy

When Howard interviewed us, Becky said, 'How you deal with discouragement is greatly determined by your temperament. I'm more passive and tend to withdraw and hide, while I've seen others become increasingly active and busy, trying to fix things and make them better on their own until they eventually burn out.

'I think my tendency to withdraw had much to do with my early home life. Growing up, my family experienced a lot of tragedy. I had three siblings die, one of which was my sister, who died in an accident when I was looking after her. She was five, and I was thirteen. As a result, I learned to self-protect, to be self-sufficient and self-contained. I carried a heavy burden of guilt, disappointment and grief until I allowed God, in His goodness, to set me free.

'I've also been through seasons when I've found church ministry discouraging, especially when it felt like I was trapped, often stuck at home, caring for a child I, of course, loved but who couldn't give a lot of the positive feedback you usually receive as a parent, like seeing developmental steps being taken.'

Ministry pressures

I, Paul, talked about how I'd managed for years to 'keep lots of plates spinning' in life, moving from one urgent and important task to the next. Then, during the pandemic, all the plates fell to the ground simultaneously! It felt impossible to give proper attention to any single issue because they all demanded my focus at the same time. The pressure on our family also intensified as the ministry challenges demanded more and more.

In all that we've gone through before with the church and our family, I would say that 2022 – not *during* the pandemic but *coming out of it* – was the season in which I felt the most discouraged. Church was challenging, as it had been everywhere. People had moved on. Others had issues brought to the surface due to the additional stress of COVID-19. Leading the New Wine movement in that season was challenging, with a dispersed leadership doing everything online for a long time, alongside the financial pressures of not having our annual gatherings. Some difficult decisions had to be made without being able to meet face to face, and a few of these decisions touched on people's futures, requiring confidentiality. This became very isolating and only increased the burden.

Personally, from my experience and talking to other leaders, I think people are tired and don't realise how worn out they are. There are a lot of leaders who haven't had the time off they need. If you think about it, it's like we went through two years of extraordinary difficulty and psychological challenge. Perhaps it will take five or more years to recover from that.

Trusting again in God's character

Reflecting on the times we've made progress detoxing discouragement, Becky shared, 'It may sound trite, but for me, only clinging to the goodness of God will get you through – trusting in His faithfulness despite the circumstances.

'We can draw three conclusions when things aren't going well. One is that God doesn't exist. Another is that God does exist, but He's not as good as He says. The last is that God is the good God He says He is in the Bible. I found that I couldn't say God doesn't exist because I'd known Him too long. But because of my past, I was susceptible to the second conclusion. I'd sometimes thought God was a hard-to-please taskmaster. He demanded, demanded and demanded. But I know now that that stemmed more from my brokenness and the pressures placed on me by some people in the church, rather than what God truly desired of me. In the end, I was able to conclude that God is good, and He knows better, and maybe I have to toughen up and deal with the fact that I'm not going to please everybody and be a perfect vicar's wife – that it's OK just to be myself.'

Worship and support

Becky continued, 'A really significant route out of discouragement for me has been worship. It helped me regain God's perspective on the difficult circumstances we faced. Worship expresses faith. It declares God is good and allows Him to move in our circumstances. It's a great resource and antidote to discouragement and self-pity.

'When we feel God has let us down or we hold Him responsible for our pain, we're much less likely to turn to Him and let Him be our resource for healing. So you've got to sort out where God is at work in your circumstances, recognising the enemy's part is to steal, kill, and destroy,[19] and God's is to redeem and give life.

---

[19] John 10:10.

'Often, when we're discouraged, we're just weary, and we need someone else to stand with us, pray for us, and say, 'It's OK; it's going to get better.' Sometimes, we'll need skilled help from a counsellor to understand how our emotional baggage affects our perspective. And some will need medical help to regain control of their thought processes.'

The hidden harvest

One scripture Becky said had been particularly helpful for her was Galatians 6:9: 'Let us not become weary in doing good, for at the proper time we will reap a harvest if we do not give up.'

She explained, 'I'm pretty prone to quitting, so I find this a helpful reminder to keep going, trusting in God that the seed hidden in the ground will bear fruit. We can't take the outward journey of ministry and fruitfulness without the hidden inward journey of healing and transformation.'

Becky finished by saying, 'It's not enough to speak God's truth, like Galatians 6:9, once or twice. You have to take it like medicine, using it repeatedly, filling yourself with the truth of God's love for you. For me, Scripture has also always been a huge comfort, not least because the writers are so honest. If we simply start reading, we can soon find something that echoes our own experience.'

Vulnerable victory

I think perhaps the most emotionally vulnerable talk I've ever given was the one I delivered at the start of the New Wine 2022 summer conference. It was a particularly challenging season, and a battle just to get to the point where the conferences could go ahead. The financial legacy of the pandemic was becoming ever more apparent. There was a real sense these could be the final gatherings and, certainly, radical changes would be needed to ensure our continued existence as a movement. In such situations, many voices and various criticisms start to be aired. Without being certain of what changes would be needed, there was a dawning realisation for me that, for New Wine to go forward, dearly loved friends on the staff team would probably lose their jobs. Looking back now, I took some of it personally, perhaps taking too much responsibility for everything.

I preached on a favourite and personally significant verse, Isaiah 49:2:

> He made my mouth like a sharpened sword,
> in the shadow of his hand he hid me;
> he made me into a polished arrow
> and concealed me in his quiver.

It's about being humble, trusting God, and being prepared in obscurity. But I was struck for the first time that the servant said, 'I have laboured in vain; I have spent my strength for nothing at all' (Isaiah 49:4). That was where I was, emotionally. It's hard to feel things might fail while you're in charge. Yet we know that the passage ends with promise and bright hope. I wonder how often, as God's servants, we miss the positive future that He has for us because we're mired in discouragement and simply give up.

But discouragement is nothing new. Saints of every age have been through this. Just as Elijah had to take a break, be fed and watered and journey to a mountain to meet with God, let God lead you. There is wisdom in the Bible and wisdom in the experience of fellow servants today.

Listen to their stories as you read the rest of this precious book, and you, too, will be restored and reappointed.

2
Why, my soul, are you downcast?

'Why' questions come with a cautionary note. As coaches, we're advised to limit our use of them because they can appear judgemental, like, 'Why did you do it?' This highlights the intimate and personal nature of the question, 'Why?' It penetrates beneath the surface. How much more so when its subject matter is our souls? It is the repeated question of Psalms 42 and 43: 'Why, my soul, are you downcast?'[20] We could paraphrase it as, 'Why is my inner self melting away?'

Within this question, there are three facets we'll explore together:

- Emotional constipation

- Internal conversation

- Spiritual evaluation

1. Emotional constipation

When faced with this question, my initial inclination is to painfully dissect myself in search of a meaningful diagnosis. I've discovered, though, that this cognitive

---

[20] Psalm 42:5, 11; 43:5.

approach often leads to spiritual constipation. Dr Bessel van der Kolk, a leading expert on traumatic stress, says trauma interferes with our ability to think clearly: 'the rational brain is basically impotent to talk the emotional brain out of its own reality'.[21] That's why I see 'why' questions working a little like laxatives, clearing out some of the emotional angst so our brains can think a bit better.

The psalmist, I believe, was questioning himself while also crying out *to* God. The possibility of him dialoguing with God about his soul melting away becomes probable in the light of his additional 'why' questions: 'Why have you forgotten [or rejected] me?' 'Why must I go about mourning, oppressed by the enemy?' (Psalms 42:9; 43:2). It's super-important to make clear who he was talking to. Psalm 42:9 begins, 'I say to God my Rock.' I think we can conclude from this that we have a holy precedent for expressing our emotional turmoil, which discouragement often brings, through a series of 'why' questions.

It's often stated that the longest journey in the world is the short distance of about eighteen inches from our head to our heart. We tend to perceive this as a top-down process, where we try to think our way into feeling. However, what if it's also a bottom-up journey? What if our comprehension of God is limited because we haven't allowed ourselves to fully experience His presence by genuinely sharing what's truly happening within us?

It may seem irrational to conceal our emotions from a loving God who discerns them even from a distance,[22] but

---

[21] Bessel van der Kolk, *The Body Keeps the Score: Brain, Mind, and Body in the Healing of Trauma*, London: Penguin, 2014, pp 55, 69.
[22] Psalm 139:2.

we have our reasons. We might find ourselves hesitant to doubt God and reluctant to blame Him because, intellectually, we know He's the epitome of goodness and not the source of evil. The knock-on effect is that we can suppress our feelings and become emotionally constipated. But what if God desires us to acknowledge and express our emotions to Him to foster a deeper connection with Him?

In her encouraging article, 'God Loves a Complainer', Laura Andrews explains away many of our reasons for staying silent:[23]

- **Fearing our experience of pain isn't bad enough because others have it worse.** But God cares about the big and small things in our lives.[24] Andrews wrote: 'I haven't found a single place in Scripture where God points to another's misfortune in order to shame us into silence about our own.' '[T]rials of various kinds' are valid (James 1:2, ESV).

- **Thinking 'it's better to wait to approach God until our faith is stronger rather than approaching him with a double mind', ie, one full of doubts.** But we are encouraged to pray: 'I do believe; help me overcome my unbelief!' (Mark 9:24).

- **Feeling too tired to find the right words to say.** But even when we don't know how to pray, 'the Spirit helps us in our weakness … [he] himself intercedes for us through wordless groans' (Romans 8:26).

---

[23] Laura Andrews, 'God Loves a Complainer,' *Journal of Biblical Counselling* 36, no 3, 2022, pp 27-37, 30.
[24] Luke 12:6-7.

- **Believing we should 'Do everything without grumbling or arguing' (Philippians 2:14).** That kind of grumbling, like the Israelites in the wilderness, is wrong. It's similar to someone slandering a friend behind their back – it's full of pride and lacks vulnerability. Yet God doesn't reject all questioning; in fact, in Jeremiah 2:6, 8 He challenges His people for not asking, 'Where is the LORD?' Why? Because such a question, when asked in faith, reflects trust in His sovereign goodness. Andrews argues that we should follow the example of Jesus, who humbly cried out His complaint from the cross with the words of Psalm 22:1, 'My God, my God, *why* have you forsaken me?' (emphasis mine).

Pause!

What 'why' laxatives might you find beneficial to take? Here are a few questions that help me: Why did I have to be made this way? Why did this have to happen? Why is life such a struggle? Why is there so much suffering in the world? Why are you doing nothing about this, God? Give voice now, if you can, to your why questions.

It's important to exercise caution, however, to avoid becoming trapped in a cycle of externalising our emotions. For some of us, continuously recounting our pain to God and seeking solace from others can reignite our distress. If you find yourself in this situation, consider trying tears and cultivating silence. In the next chapter, Katia Adams shares a powerful story about how she put this into practice.

2. Internal conversation

Dr Martyn Lloyd-Jones, in his insightful book *Spiritual Depression*, observed that much of our unhappiness stems from 'listening to yourself instead of talking to yourself'.[25] He pointed out how negative ideas we didn't consciously choose can slip into our minds, often stirring up disappointments and past hurts. Rather than letting unwanted thoughts like these have free rein, Lloyd-Jones directs our attention to Psalm 42. Here, the psalmist proactively addressed his soul and challenged its narrative.

When the emotional fog begins to clear, we're better placed to notice this inner dialogue. We can start to understand it by paying attention to it. We can reflect on where such thoughts might come from so we can speak powerfully to them. For now, let's tune in to this inner conversation we all have. What automatic thoughts can you hear? Is there an inner critic disapprovingly putting you down? Maybe it's a mean manager demanding perfection or an overprotective firefighter trying so hard to shield you from harm that it's keeping you from things that bring joy and life.

3. Spiritual evaluation

As the storm of our emotions further subsides, we can discern three interconnected sources of discouragement: the flesh, the world and the devil.

---

[25] Martyn Lloyd-Jones, *Spiritual Depression: Its Causes and Cure*, London: Pickering & Ingliss, 1979, pp 20-21.

The flesh

The aspect of our humanity referred to as the 'flesh' represents the part of us yet to be fully renewed. It relates to our struggles with sin, especially discouragement that metastasises from repetitive wrongdoing, whatever that may be. Profound hope, however, is available, as my wife and I explored in our first book, *Spiritual Detox*,[26] focusing on the truths outlined in 1 John 1:9. God promises to generously, abundantly and repeatedly forgive *all* our sins when we confess them to Him. The turmoil caused by genuine guilt can be removed entirely as God separates us from our transgressions as far as the infinite expanse between east and west.[27] Instead of discouraging us, our sins can serve as catalysts for drawing us closer to the forgiving, encouraging heart of God.

However, there's also what Mark Meynell calls 'the curse of imagined guilt', in his insightful book, *When Darkness Seems My Closest Friend*. He describes how it often starts with some kind of wrongdoing, but it becomes inaccurately magnified as we replay the moment repeatedly in our minds. When we're feeling down or depressed, these mental reruns can make the 'guilt' seem overwhelming. It can be most unsettling, though, when there's no clear reason for the guilt at all. We stand in the

---

[26] Howard and Holly Satterthwaite, *Spiritual Detox: Discovering the Joy of Liberating Confession*, London: SPCK, 2021.
[27] Psalm 103:12.

dock, and 'plead guilty to all charges, even when the charge sheet is blank'.[28]

In such situations, says Meynell, we need good friends like Katniss Everdeen who, towards the end of *The Hunger Games* series, helped Peeta Mellark. He'd been horribly tortured with mind-altering drugs to twist his understanding of everything, including who his real friends were; he even turned on Katniss. But she patiently helped him recognise their true bond, reminding him how they've always remained committed to protecting each other.[29]

Pause!

We all need this reality reference point, especially when we're fighting phantom guilt. Take a moment to think about who this could be for you. How could you strengthen that relationship today?

As much as we should be mindful of our 'spiritual' flesh, we should also be aware of our 'physical' flesh and how they can interact. Perhaps surprisingly for some, Dr Martyn Lloyd-Jones began his exploration of the causes and cure of spiritual depression with the essential primary consideration of a person's temperament and physical conditions. Just as we would not put every person on our planet on matching diets, Christians shouldn't be treated

---

[28] Mark Meynell, *When Darkness Seems My Closest Friend: Reflections on Life and Ministry with Depression*, London: IVP, 2008, pp 58-59.

[29] Meynell, *When Darkness*, pp 144-145. *The Hunger Games: Mockingjay – Part 2*, directed by Francis Lawrence, Santa Monica, CA: Lionsgate, 2015, film.

identically. He believed certain people were particularly vulnerable to spiritual depression, especially when they were physically weak. Encouragingly, he said, 'I could make out a good case for saying that quite often, the people who stand out most gloriously in the history of the Church are people of the very type we are now considering.'[30]

It's vital, then, that we take note of how physical factors, like exhaustion from overworking or frustration from getting old and flabby, can make us more susceptible to discouragement. We mustn't separate the physical from the spiritual – they're deeply connected.

Recognising our vulnerability, however, isn't about making excuses or dodging responsibility. Instead, it's about gaining a deeper self-awareness that empowers us to take better care of our physical needs, to be kinder in the way we talk to ourselves and to shut down those unhelpful, critical voices that only drag us down.

Nobody's perfect – far from it. Even the apostle Paul dealt with what he called a 'thorn in my flesh'. Some speculate it might have related to mental health challenges. Whatever it was, it turned from irritation to invitation. Through this hardship, Paul discovered the sufficiency of God's grace. His struggles became a stage for God's power to shine through his 'weaknesses' (2 Corinthians 12:7-10). How amazing is that?

The world

Our world is full of God-given beauty, but it's also, as the English poet Lord Alfred Tennyson put it, 'red in tooth

---

[30] Lloyd-Jones, *Spiritual Depression*, pp 16-17.

and claw'.[31] This 'good'[32] created world now groans under the destructive effects of sin emanating from rebellion in the Garden of Eden. As a result, many of us are discouraged and even traumatised because we've been sinned against emotionally, physically or sexually. We've faced deep disappointments, such as children or close friends walking away from God. Or we've endured tragic accidents, natural disasters, conflict and even war.

It's worth pointing out that it doesn't have to be one 'big' thing, either. The accumulation of lots of 'small' to 'medium' things can grind us down. Grief, loss, heartache and pain are an unavoidable part of the human story. They leave behind a mark that can weaken our spirits and make us vulnerable to future discouragement.

Perhaps what I've learned about myself here might help. I was hospitalised for four days, aged three, for a near-fatal asthma attack. I was unknowingly traumatised with a profound sense of feeling unsafe in my own skin. Or, as Rachael Newham described her own breathing difficulties following a psychiatrist's assessment: 'I had grown up with a sense that my body could not be trusted.'[33] This was amplified for me with a dyslexia diagnosis at age seven and severe migraines and irritating eczema caused by allergies to wheat and dairy at age eight. Together, they paved the way for unsatisfying plastic surgery to make myself more acceptable at age

---

[31] Alfred Tennyson, *In Memoriam A.H.H.*, London: Edward Moxon, 1850, canto 56.

[32] Genesis 1:4, 10, 12, 18, 21, 25, 31.

[33] Rachael Newham, *Learning to Breathe: My Journey with Mental Illness*, London: SPCK, 2018, p 14.

nineteen and a subsequent diagnosis of body dysmorphic disorder – outworkings of a deeply entrenched sense of not being good enough. However, I didn't grasp the significance of this until my early forties, thanks to quality time with a gifted Christian counsellor.

Pause!

What past or present pains – big or small – have shaped your sense of safety, wellbeing and worth? How could you invite God – and trusted others – into those areas for deeper healing?

According to pastor and author John Mark Comer, the world can be understood as a comprehensive corrupted framework encompassing 'ideas, values, morals, practices and societal norms'.[34] It's an echo chamber for evil. Through various communication channels, it promotes unattainable ideals of 'the good life' and intensifies fears of missing out if we don't pursue them wholeheartedly.

So often the world imposes excessive demands, resembling a cruel taskmaster akin to the Egyptian pharaoh, relentlessly driving us to work harder.[35] It repeats the capitalist mantra of our era: 'More, more, more.' Deceptively, it promises we can have it all – a happy family, a luxurious home and a successful career. Yet, in reality, this relentless bricks-without-straw pursuit can all to easily leave us broken, struggling to accept our human limitations. The world promotes unrealistic

---

[34] John Mark Comer, *Live No Lies: Recognize and Resist the Three Enemies that Sabotage Your Peace*, London: SPCK, 2021, p 242.
[35] See Exodus 5.

expectations that inevitably lead to our downfall. Instead, we should embrace the gift of limits God offers because, as Peter Scazzero, co-founder of Emotionally Healthy Discipleship, encourages, 'They keep us grounded and humble, reminding us we are not in charge of running the world.'[36] In the words of anxiety management guru Steve Cuss, let us learn to 'be human sized instead of always trying to be superhuman'.[37]

If, on the one hand, the world is unreasonably demanding, on the other, it's unduly mollycoddling. Here, the image is the proverbial adulteress's sweet words: 'With persuasive words she led him astray; she seduced him with her smooth talk' (Proverbs 7:21). Like the seductive sirens of Greek mythology, it encourages us to indulge in every desire, believing we deserve it, as if pleasure is the ultimate goal. This path of self-indulgence, however, leads to self-absorption, diminishing our sense of purpose, achievement, significance and meaning. When we become consumed by personal gratification, the joy of giving and serving others gets overshadowed, leaving us (if you're anything like me) feeling flabby and unfulfilled.

Believing one of these 'we can have it all' false paths will inevitably leave us discouraged.

---

[36] Peter Scazzero, *Emotionally Healthy Discipleship: Moving from Shallow Christianity to Deep Transformation*, Grand Rapids, MI: Zondervan, 2021, pp 96-97. www.emotionallyhealthy.org (accessed 9th April 2025).

[37] 'The Counterintuitive Lesson of Caring for Yourself First', *Christianity Today*, July 2024, www.christianitytoday.com/2024/07/caring-for-yourself-first-wellness-psychology-therapy-grief (accessed 30th May 2025).

The devil

There's a tale of unknown origin that's often shared about the devil's inventory of destructive tools. Hatred, envy, deceit, lust and pride: each tool was priced according to its perceived worth and displayed on a table. However, one stood out, showing signs of significant wear and tear. Intrigued, a curious observer picked it up, examined it closely and noticed its exorbitant price tag. Perplexed, they asked, 'Why is this tool more costly than the others?'

In response, the devil laughed and replied, 'Ah, that is the tool known as discouragement. It holds unparalleled power among all my instruments. With it, I can pry open a person's heart and then employ my other tools to their full extent. Hence, it demands a higher price.'

The devil is the 'father of lies' who 'prowls', 'schemes' and discouragingly 'accuses' (John 8:44; 1 Peter 5:8; Ephesians 6:11; Revelation 12:10). Discouragement is commonplace because of his existence. Do not underestimate his ability to kill your courage. We must stay alert to his evil work so we don't get outwitted by him (2 Corinthians 2:11). This can happen when we align ourselves with one of his typical tactics, telling ourselves we're worthless. No! Resist this poison. The cross declares, 'We are precious!'

Note also that the devil won't give us a break because we're having a difficult day or had a challenging childhood. He's partial, not impartial like our good God. He'll exploit everything he can. So cut yourself some slack. We're combatants in a very real and vicious war. It's OK, normal, right even, to feel battle weary.

We may have fleshly frailties and sometimes succumb to worldly wisdom, but we can still stand firm against the devil, even as he seeks to take advantage of them. God has given us agency. We can stand firm in the armour of God, the glorious attributes of God Himself.[38] He gives us His authority to speak to our souls, like the psalmist, and to stop listening to ourselves, the world and the devil. He encourages us to tell ourselves the only safe place where we can put our hope. But before we do, let's stop and think.

Stop and think

- How can you graciously acknowledge the valid reasons (the flesh, the world and the devil) for your weariness while still inviting God's restorative hope and compassion into those very places?

- Which of the world's lies are you more tempted to buy into and why – its exhausting demands of 'more' or its self-indulgence siren song? How is this affecting your sense of purpose and wholeness?

- Where have you noticed the devil's voice of discouragement prying open your heart to more of his poison?

---

[38] Ephesians 6:10-20.

3
Try tears
Katia Adams

Katia is a director of the ministry Frequentsee and the founding pastor of The Table Boston (a church in the heart of Boston, Massachusetts). She was born in the Middle East and inherited a legacy of revival from her grandparents and parents, who are leading pioneers of the modern-day church in Iran. In addition to being a preacher, pastor and international speaker, she's a medical doctor, wife to Julian Adams, mother to two busy children and author of Equal *(Colorado Springs, CO: David C Cook, 2020). For more information, visit www.katiaadams.org*

Discouragement sapped my strength

When I've been discouraged, beyond the general negative emotions that are sometimes associated with the word, I have found myself more literally sapped of the courage I've needed to keep going; a disarming of my strength. Sadness and frustration have, of course, been present within the experience, but underpinning those emotions has been the sense that I didn't have it in me to keep doing what I was called to do.

A series of challenges

The greatest times of discouragement that I've experienced have not stemmed from one large catastrophic event, but a series of smaller, back-to-back challenges. A few years ago, my husband and I found ourselves facing significant financial strain. We'd spent two years with sporadic income planting a church in an expensive city. At one point, neither of us had any earnings. Due to COVID-19, we were unable to travel to speak at conferences, and the financial plan we'd been relying on disappeared overnight. We were left living off our savings. It was a scary, unnerving season. But just as we grappled with our loss of income and stretched finances, another issue arose.

Our landlord announced he was selling our home, forcing us to move. The problems were mounting up. We looked at rentals and realised we couldn't afford to live in the city we had come to serve. All the financially feasible options before us meant we would have a gruelling hour-and-a-half commute to both the church plant and our children's schools. For about six weeks, we lived with the unsettling thought, 'We have nowhere to go.'

Then we had a miraculous moment: someone gifted us the money we needed for a deposit to buy a house in the city. It was a crazy turnaround. We put in an offer on a home, and everything seemed to be going ahead. Then, at the last minute, the bank pulled out of the mortgage and it seemed we would lose the house. Suddenly there was a massive amount of pressure on top of us again.

After a tense few weeks, we finally managed to secure another mortgage in order to buy the house. A wonderful moment of breakthrough, we thought! But three days after we moved in, our new house flooded, destroying two floors and most of our furniture. We immediately had to move out into temporary housing.

Months of stress followed, including battling our insurance company to make good. Was any of it like a horrific illness or loss of life? No, not at all. But it was six months of tension, heartache and disappointment. A season of thinking God would do something, even thinking God had done something, only to walk into increased difficulty.

A crisis of calling

'I'm done; I can't do this,' I said. In the midst of it all, while trying to keep things stable for our two young children in a tiny apartment that we were fighting with our insurance company to pay for, I had a meltdown with God. I felt so discouraged and angry. 'I can't put my kids through this,' I thought.

As I tried to make sense of what was happening that summer, I kept telling God, 'It can't be that You're not good and faithful... but why, then, are You letting all of this happen?' After my initial outbursts – where I admitted, 'I love You, but right now I don't even like You' – my thoughts shifted to a deeper crisis: 'When I'm having such a crisis of confidence in God, how can I possibly continue as a pastor?'

This is one of the unique challenges for church leaders that I think many people don't recognise. Life doesn't simply continue for us in an ordinary work context; it unfolds in an environment where you're responsible for guiding other people's faith journeys. Even when you're at your lowest, wrestling with your own questions about God,

Sunday comes around and you're back in front of the congregation, preaching.

What discouraged me most was whether I'd misunderstood God in all the moments where I'd felt He'd led us to our house. It made me question, 'Do I genuinely hear Him right?' 'Do I know Him as well as I think?' I particularly felt the pressures of these questions while leading a community based on what I think God's saying – even though I know I'm not figuring it out alone, and others are helping me listen, too. Should I be leading a church if I'm not a good judge of His voice?

At that time, God spoke to me and challenged me to find someone in Scripture who had wrestled with feelings of hurt and disappointment like me, and to learn from them. Like many, I found Elijah. We became friends and I studied him for about six weeks. It was so healing and cathartic to walk through his anger and discouragement and say, 'Yep, I'm totally with you.'

What does the church really need?

I remember talking with Julian, my husband, and saying, 'I can't possibly be what the church needs right now.'

God bless godly spouses because Julian replied, 'That's funny; I wonder what you think the church needs, then?'

As I started thinking through this, I began to see that a pastor journeying through disappointment was exactly what the church needed in that season. I could be a guidebook on how to walk with Jesus through painful seasons. If church leaders like me don't model how to come through these times still believing, we'll be left with a generation that deconstructs because they've only had 'success story' models. The average Christian isn't living their own success story. They're living through trials of various kinds, but most haven't had anyone provide a guide map for them.

Of course, this wasn't quite so well thought through at the time. But looking back, I can see what God was doing in and through me during that season, and why it was so good for the church. It was a beautiful time for our community. So many people felt permission to process their pain, and offence against God was brought into the light and healed. It seemed like our roots suddenly went down twenty feet deeper overnight.

Doubts are inevitable

I've since realised that much of the faith deconstruction people experience begins when they reach a breaking point of pain. As they grapple with disappointment, they often conclude that their doubts are incompatible with following Jesus, rather than seeing them as an inevitable part of the faith journey. There are so many different strands that weave together to create the deconstruction moment – and I'm not trying to belittle that in any way. Some people experience hardships so much more challenging than mine. But the more I walk through seasons of discouragement, the more I realise that they are not anomalous to faith. The Bible has much to say to us not only in those seasons, but in also warning us of those seasons. I've begun to say to myself and to our community, 'We have to read the fine print when it comes to a life of faith.' In our often-rushed devotional times, many of us read to find a verse that blesses us rather than reading to allow Scripture to train us for storms. I wonder if perhaps our devotional times need an overhaul?

A great running buddy

As a college student, I went through a few years of loving running. I found I could keep going if I had someone running with me more than if I was on my own. That's just everyday life, right? In my season of housing disappointment, Julian was my spiritual running buddy. He ran alongside me at a pace my painful legs could carry while ensuring I was still going forward.

I think that we have to be careful who we choose to be around us in seasons of discouragement. Some of us gravitate towards people who will nurture our pain, validate it in and of itself and treat it as a destination, rather than finding a wise pacesetter to run alongside us. I'm not talking about finding someone who just quotes verses at you; that's like someone running miles ahead and can be unhelpful and discouraging in itself. What we need is someone with the sensitivity to follow at our reduced pace without allowing us to give up – that's what Julian did for me. He didn't belittle my pain or unhelpfully let me get stuck in it. He said, 'This is horrible right now. I'll help you get through it to the other side.'

Crying out without words

As a feisty Middle Easterner, when I'm frustrated, a lot can come out of me that's not particularly helpful or necessarily true, but I need to get it out. In this season of discouragement, however, after the first couple of weeks of doing that with God, I found it was actually hurting me more than it was helping. It wasn't like I had a finite amount of words and then it was out. I realised, 'Oh, no, my hurt is just multiplying.'

Now, I'm not saying this is for everyone, but what really helped me was having prayer times where I said nothing and, if I'm honest, thought nothing. I'd say, 'Hey, God, this is me praying today, OK?' I harnessed my mouth, put worship music on, let it wash over me, and cried. I cried out the disappointment. I cried out the hurt.

I found this one of the most healing parts of the journey. God showed up. It's not that I heard Him say anything spectacular; I just found it incredibly healing to be still and allow the atmosphere of worship to bring restoration.

After maybe a month or two, I sensed courage returning. I started to see God at work in this horrible, frustrating situation. I saw growth in me, and in others around me.

Crying permitted the unwanted emotions to seep out. They were getting out of my body rather than being caught in a vicious cycle of replenishment within me. For some of you who might feel stuck in the cycle of processing pain, I trust that trying tears in the context of worship might be equally healing for you, too.

Discouragement is not unusual

In closing, discouragement isn't unusual, and can even be profitable if we're able to process it. If we can view moments of pain and disappointment as opportunities for encounter and growth, it can alleviate some of the hopelessness these seasons bring. If we can view doubts and struggles as part and parcel of a life of faith, it can dissipate some of the isolation and shame. It enables us to learn from these experiences and move forward rather than feeling we have to sit out the rest of the race. We don't!

4

Where is your hope?

Have you ever stopped to think about how often you lose things? Well, according to a survey of 3,000 adults, the average person misplaces up to nine items every single day.[39] Yes, nine! We're talking about the usual suspects – phones, bank cards and car keys. Sound familiar? It's estimated that we spend about ten minutes a day trying to hunt them down.

There's a far more significant loss, however, that can consume way more time. It is, of course, the loss of hope. It reminds me of a story about Mary and Joseph in Luke 2:41-52. They managed to misplace something (or rather Someone) super-important – their twelve-year-old son, Jesus! Can you imagine? They were heading home from Jerusalem and didn't realise until after a day's journey that Jesus, the embodiment of hope, wasn't with them. Talk about panic mode. But isn't this a challenging representation of what we can do with hope?

---

[39] 'Lost something already today? Misplaced items cost us ten minutes a day', *Daily Mail*, www.dailymail.co.uk/news/article-2117987/Lost-today-Misplaced-items-cost-minutes-day.html (accessed 3rd December 2024).

Shortly after the psalmist questioned himself, he spoke to himself, 'Put your hope in God' (Psalm 42:5, 11; Psalm 43:5). We should take note of this because it means we can misplace hope, discouraging ourselves by putting it in things other than God.

Did you also notice how the psalmist didn't wait for hope to appear? He took action: 'Put.' It's almost as if he was reminding himself – and us – that hope requires intentionality. The New Testament mirrors this 'put' language on numerous occasions,[40] encouraging us to *set* our hope on God and to *hold on* to it 'unswervingly' (Hebrews 10:23). To accomplish this, it's crucial we discern the difference between true and false hope.

False hope

There are many false hopes out there we can foolishly put faith in, from get-rich-quick schemes to miracle anti-ageing products. Most of us are alert to such scams. Instead, it's the half-truth hopes that cleverly camouflage themselves as the real deal we can get conned by.

One Christmas, I was invited to speak at the Lawyers' Christian Fellowship (LCF) carol service at St Botolph's in the city of London. I arrived early, only to stumble across another carol service unexpectedly underway. I contacted the LCF organiser, who kindly said I was at the wrong church. It turned out the correct venue was a different St Botolph's, not St Botolph's-without-Bishopsgate. Seeking a solution, I called for a taxi, and the driver took me to another St Botolph's, but unfortunately, it was also the wrong one. The right venue wasn't St Botolph's without

---

[40] 1 Timothy 4:10; 1 Timothy 6:17; 1 Peter 3:5.

Aldgate, either. In the nick of time, I eventually arrived to preach at St Botolph's-without-Aldersgate.

Finding the correct address of hope can be even more challenging. Counterfeit hopes capitalise on our yearning for desirable and not necessarily bad things like wealth, intimacy and success. Money can bring a sense of security, sex can be fulfilling and career success can offer a powerful sense of accomplishment. And yes, God does desire to bless, provide for and care for His children. But here's where things can go off track: these truths sometimes give rise to false hopes. They can seed unreal expectations that we should always be materially wealthy and free from hardship, enjoy perfect relationships, excel effortlessly in our careers and experience positive answers to every prayer we utter. It's not only unrealistic; it's also misleading.

If we're honest, we've all allowed at least one good thing to be turned into a god-thing in our lives. Desires that often pertain more to wants than needs can take centre stage in allocating our time, talents and treasure. But since they can't ultimately deliver the earthly paradise we long for, they breed discouragement.

Pause!

What false hopes have you been fooled by – and why? What drew you in, and how did they ultimately let you down? Looking back, what do you think you were really hoping for, and how might you discover a deeper, more fulfilling answer to that desire in God?

Empty havens

When David was on the run from Saul, he sought solace in all sorts of ways. First, it was through his relationship with the prophet Samuel. It provided temporary relief but didn't deliver him from Saul's murderous ambitions. Next, he turned to his loyal friend, Jonathan, Saul's son. He, however, was unable to protect David from his tyrannical father. David then sought refuge with Ahimelech, the chief priest, and even obtained Goliath's sword, perhaps to give a tangible sense of victory, but they didn't give the comfort he yearned for either. Desperate, he resorted to seeking assistance from the Philistines, an ancient enemy of his people; only, it led to him dribbling into his beard like a madman.[41]

I'll be honest – there have been many moments when I've misplaced hope. I've sought to put it in things that couldn't possibly carry the weight, like the opinion of others. I didn't dribble into my beard, but I occasionally ended up crying inside. Maybe you've been there too – feeling let down or even a little lost. Let's find out how we can avoid this by unpacking what David did in the pivotal verse 1 Samuel 30:6.

In the Lord

It seems David underwent a significant transformation. Rather than seeking encouragement solely from a church leader or relying on the support of a close friend, David primarily found solace 'in the LORD'. He did not place his confidence in his own abilities, as modern pop culture

---

[41] 1 Samuel 19:18-24; 20; 21:1-9, 10-15.

often suggests, with its 'look for the hero within' focus, which can be challenging when we feel discouraged by our perceived inadequacies. Instead, David derived strength from the Lord. This is the profound source of genuine, steadfast hope.

The author of the book of Hebrews said true hope is not a maybe hope. It's an 'anchor for the soul, firm and secure' (Hebrews 6:19). An anchor, as we all know, prevents a ship from losing its way, particularly during storms. Historically, they comprised baskets filled with stones or sacks of sand, leveraging weight and friction against the sea floor to keep a vessel in place.

True hope is 'firm and secure' because it's unbreakably chained to our gloriously weighty and unchanging God. This is no dead weight. It's a 'living hope' (1 Peter 1:3) that actively imparts life, and from it 'faith and love' spring up (Colossians 1:5). It is the 'hope of glory' (Colossians 1:27). The hope that we will revel in glorified bodies, residing eternally in a beautifully renewed creation, in intimate communion with God – not if, but when. We have incredible treasure stored up for us! Knowing this restores courage to our inner beings, as Paul wrote: 'Therefore, since we have such a hope, we are very bold' (2 Corinthians 3:12).

Pause!

True hope tastes the first fruits of new life in the present while anticipating the fulfilment feast in eternity. It's been said some of us are too heavenly minded to be of much earthly good. These days, I think it's more often the other way around. Professor C S Lewis would agree. He said the most impactful

Christians in this world were the ones who spent more time thinking about the next.[42] So which way do you lean – and why?

Look in the right direction

If we live with a clearer vision of our amazing, eternal future, we'll be considerably less discouraged in the present. The way to cultivate this, of course, is to persistently look in the right direction. Abraham, Peter and Mary Magdalene are helpful examples. Each of them found it hard at times to see God's bigger picture and felt overwhelmed, yet their stories remind us that these times can bring about growth. We're encouraged not just by their struggles, but also by how they learned to look in the right direction.

Abraham

In Genesis 15:1-6, we find one of the great fathers of the faith, Abraham, discouraged. He must have been exhausted from the preceding battle. Moreover, a significant amount of time had passed since God promised him a child. But there was no pregnancy in sight. Seemingly blind to the miraculous, against-the-odds victory God had just given him, Abraham was looking down on his present circumstances. 'How can I have a child?' I imagine him asking in his weariness. 'How can my family line be a blessing to all peoples on the earth?[43] It's impossible, God!'

---

[42] C S Lewis, *Mere Christianity*, London: Fount, 1997, p 111.
[43] Genesis 12:2-3.

So often, we're tempted to think mature faith means not talking to God like this. But Abraham models bringing his complaint to God. God spoke as Abraham contemplated human solutions, like appointing his servant, Eliezer, as his heir. He took Abraham outside and said, '"Look up at the sky and count the stars – if indeed you can count them." Then he said to him, "So shall your offspring be"' (Genesis 15:5).

God wants us to spend more time looking up to get His higher, heavenly perspective. Why? Because if we keep looking down on ourselves and our circumstances, we'll get discouraged. But we'll be encouraged when we look up to God, remember His promises and see His power. When God spoke to Abraham, He not only reminded him of His promise but also showcased His power. It's easily overlooked, just like the casual 'also made the stars' comment in the creation narrative (Genesis 1:16). I think God was saying, 'I want you to know that I possess the power to keep all the promises I make.'

Having spent much of my life in London, I found that genuine and metaphorical light pollution left me feeling more 'awe-stuck' than awestruck. I didn't regularly see into 'the heavens [that] declare the glory of God [and] the skies [that] proclaim the work of his hands' (Psalm 19:1). Perhaps you, like me, have experienced times when amazement at the incredible power and goodness of our Almighty God seems to fade. It's time we looked up. In our galaxy alone, it's been calculated that there are around 100 thousand million stars.[44] In Scripture, we're reminded

---

[44] European Space Agency, 'How Many Stars Are There in the Universe?', tinyurl.com/4vwyr26r (accessed 10th April 2025).

that God not only appointed the vast number of stars; He also knows each of them by name. Immediately following this revelation, the psalmist concluded, 'Great is our Lord and *mighty in power*' (Psalm 147:4-5, emphasis mine).

Like Abraham, sometimes we just need to step outside and look up at the stars – to remember that the One who holds the universe together also holds us.

Peter

God gave Peter and the disciples a difficult task: to row through the night, after an exhausting day, into conditions that blew up into a storm.[45] Sometimes, God sanctifies us by permitting us to undergo challenging, even discouraging, situations. However, we're never alone in them. Jesus saw the disciples struggling in the dark as they strained at the oars – despite them being in the middle of a 13km-wide lake. Our God is the God who sees – *El Roi* – the same God who witnessed the distress of Hagar and came to her aid in her time of need, as we read in Genesis 16.

The passage, intriguingly, mentions that Jesus intended to 'pass by' the disciples (Mark 6:48). To grasp the meaning, we need to interpret it through the lens of Exodus 33:18-19 when Moses implored God to show him His glory: God responded by causing all His goodness to 'pass in front of [Moses]', revealing His nature. 'The LORD, the LORD, the compassionate and gracious God, slow to anger, abounding in love and faithfulness' (Exodus 34:6).

Jesus knew that what the disciples needed more than practical help was powerful hope, ignited by a clearer

---

45 Matthew 14:22-24; Mark 6:45-52.

vision of Him walking on water. When life gets tough, we need to see God: His supernatural power and glory. Then, in seeing Him, we should do what He says, 'Take courage!' (Matthew 14:27).

As we look to Jesus, like Peter we'll hear Him say, 'Come' (Matthew 14:29). It's like He's saying, 'Join Me in victory over the satanic sea-disturbing enemy.' And as long as we keep our eyes fixed on Him, we won't escape troubles, but we'll be able to walk through them with Him. How do we put our hope in God? By 'fixing our eyes on Jesus' (Hebrews 12:2) and beholding the Lord.[46]

Our challenge, however, lies in our susceptibility to distractions. Instead of looking to Him, like Peter we find ourselves drawn to the storm, the figurative wind and waves, whether external pressures or inner critics. We become fixated on the very things that breed discouragement, leading us to sink beneath their weight. But wonderfully, as Peter began to submerge, Jesus *immediately* reached out to rescue him.

Mary
Mary wept. All she could see was death, even though there were mysterious clues to resurrection life: an empty tomb and angels in white. She'd come to honour her fallen hero, but assumed someone had taken His body. How could anybody do such a thing? But then a voice and two questions came forth, followed by her name, tenderly spoken, 'Mary' (John 20:15-16). Only one person had ever uttered her name with such sacred affection. At that moment, she turned and beheld the man addressing her,

---

[46] 2 Corinthians 3:18.

realising that he was no ordinary gardener – it was Jesus, alive! Mary's tears previously flowed because she'd been looking in the wrong direction, not perceiving the resurrection hope beside her.

Seeing Jesus changed everything. In Him, she glimpsed the new creation: what happened to Jesus' glorified body will one day happen to all things. No wonder she tried to cling to Him, yearning for that fulfilment now – for everything evil to come undone.

When we fix our eyes upon Jesus, we also set our sights on the glorious new heaven and earth that await us. It gives perspective, helping us see that our troubles are 'light and momentary' compared with the weighty glory of eternity (2 Corinthians 4:13-18). That's not to dismiss our discouragements. Paul's point is that even martyrdom is like one night spent in a bad hotel compared to the glorious good that's coming. My wife, Holly, and I once spent an evening in a Lanzarote guest house crawling with cockroaches – even under the pillows! But the next week, in a gorgeous apartment, basking in the sun by the pool, with wine and chocolates, we forgot that dreadful first day entirely. How much more will the new heaven and earth overshadow our present struggles?

A day is coming when all things will be made new – no sin, sickness, suffering, or death. We'll enjoy the best things, only supersized, without crime, pollution, sirens or lawyers. (I can write that because I used to be one!) It's not that they won't be there, just that most will need new jobs. The absence of conflict will mean there'll be nothing to litigate. Every wrong will already have been made right. Christians who suffer now will suffer no more. John Piper's poem 'Glorified' imagines this vividly, with pets alive again and amputees running for joy. I recommend looking it up.[47]

Turning our gaze

When I sent my poem to *Evangelicals Now*, I didn't expect a response, but to my delight, in the following month's issue, I received an encouraging, poetic charge to look to Jesus:[48]

Dear Editor,
Thank you to Pastor Anon! I hope his words helped many readers appreciate the harm that can be done by unkind criticism. They prompted me to share this, which I once had to write to myself:

Keep on, weary one,
Tempted one, keep on!

You're not doing it for 'the sweet smell of success'
Or the sweet sound of appreciation tickling the ear!
You only have one Boss,
One ultimate Director.
He knows why you're doing it,
And why you're needed here.

Keep on, weary one,
Lonely, tested one. *Keep on!*

You're not a poor abandoned man
Just wishing he was blessed.

[47] John Piper, 'Glorified', 1985, www.desiringgod.org/articles/glorified (accessed 13th February 2025).
[48] Letter to the Editor, November 2022.

You're not a failing salesperson
Trying… his… best…

Remember who you do it for.
Remember who you do it with.
The One whose eyes are on you now!
The One who went for you
To death!

He was once the weary One.
The tempted, the rejected One.
But He kept on…
He *still* keeps on
Till out of death comes *LIFE!*

So keep on, weary one!
Take heart, lonely one!
Look to the Holy One
And keep on
Keeping on.[49]

One powerful way we can turn our gaze upwards is by finding faith to encounter God again in His Word. The deeply discouraged Emmaus Road disciples experienced hope being fanned into flame when Jesus 'opened the Scriptures' to them (Luke 24:32). This should come as no surprise, as Paul wrote, 'everything that was written in the past was written to teach us, so that through the endurance taught in the Scriptures and the *encouragement* they provide we might have *hope*' (Romans 15:4, emphasis mine).

---

[49] Used with the kind permission of its author, Luther Chaplin.

Stop and think

- In what ways is the Christian's true hope greater than all the false hopes of this world? How can you hold on to this truth when you're tempted to find solace in empty havens?

- Abraham's Perspective: When you're discouraged, like Abraham, are you spending more time looking down at your circumstances or looking up to God's power? How could you do more of the latter?

- Peter's Distraction: Like Peter, who faltered when distracted by the storm, what 'wind and waves' in your life are taking your attention away from Jesus? How could you proactively fix your eyes back on Him and find courage again?

- Mary's Recognition: Mary's tears blinded her to the resurrection hope before her. What might cloud your vision of the hope and power of Jesus in your life today? How can you turn your gaze to see Him more clearly and embrace the joy of His presence?

5

Pursue purpose
Andy Kind

Andy Kind is a comedian, preacher and writer who has earned a living from laughter since 2005. He's smashed through 2,000 gigs, won the Anything for Laffs award, and been hailed as 'Terrific' (The Scotsman) *and a master of 'tossing out comic gems'* (The Yorkshire Times). *His comedy has graced BBC1, ITV, Channel 4,* Dave's One Night Stand *and* Live at the Apollo. *He's also penned several books, including* Hidden in Plain Sight *(Rotherham: McKnight & Bishop, 2022) and* Curious Tales of Redemption *(Rotherham: McKnight & Bishop Laugh). For more information, visit www.andykind.co.uk*

Understanding discouragement

Discouragement really means to lose courage, doesn't it? In the same way that 'enjoy' means to take joy, 'encourage' means to take courage. What often brings about discouragement, then, is not being able to see why you're doing what you're doing. Think of it like a battlefield: charging the enemy line at Gallipoli or the Somme – we believe we'll be mowed down the moment we step out of the trench. That's what discouragement feels like. It sets in when we think victory isn't possible, can't see why it matters or, to change metaphors, stop believing the referee is seeing things right. It's when we can't see the purpose, or how progress will come from what we're doing, that hopelessness invades us. Courage holds hands with hope; a loss of hope results in discouragement, which is a loss of bravery.

Losing courage in ministry and comedy

On stage, I lost courage, mainly in the early days when I'd had an awful gig (eg, having urine thrown at me by someone in the crowd). In ministry, I've felt that same discouragement. There were times when I was running a great race with others, but division crept in. Suddenly, progress stalled, and I found myself wondering, 'What's the point any more?' It can feel like the people you're leading and who are leading you don't care. Self-preservation kicks in. We start to think, 'I can't go through that again – go into a situation where I'm going to be hurt by people.' I don't mind being heckled by an unbeliever or sworn at or swindled by somebody who's not a Christian. But there is no deeper or more difficult wound to heal than one that is from a brother or sister in Christ. That's when we lose courage.

I've made some dreadful mistakes, wilfully, and haven't been a good role model for Christian living. However, that's not what discourages me most. I lose courage when it seems like the people who are supposed to be for me are actually against me, including God. That's when discouragement really kicks in, and you *feel* like you can't take it any more. I know our feelings are good servants and terrible masters, but it's still hard.

Distinguishing God's voice

I think the voice of the Father and the voice of the enemy sound quite similar if you don't know the difference. The enemy hisses, 'I know what you're really like.' God gently declares, 'I know who you truly are.' Similar words, different tone – and worlds apart in meaning. Our identity is not our behaviour. Yes, I think we must have humility. We need to be able to acknowledge where we've gotten things wrong.

But genuine repentance can often be met with condemnation – yet that's not how Jesus rolls. Peter betrayed Jesus three times, and Jesus said to him (I'm paraphrasing), 'Come and have breakfast on the beach.'

Jesus asked, 'Do you love me?'

Peter responded, 'Yes, I love you' – and he was accepted.[50] There's no precondition of Christian counselling, or any passive aggression.

Jesus simply asked, 'Are you still with me?'

Peter said, 'Yes.'

And Jesus effectively said, 'Great, well, let's go for it again.'

That's the gospel: not a kind of moralistic judgementalism where people have repented only when you feel like they have.

Society's misplaced identity

I don't think we're encouraged as a society, but I don't think we're inspired to be. Our society doesn't value bravery; it values victimhood. We're encouraged to live in our brokenness and victimhood and blame everybody else. And I think that's seeped into the Church. When

---

[50] John 21.

somebody causes you harm, they're often called an abuser, manipulative or controlling, and you're the victim. There are genuine cases where that happens, but often there's fault on both sides.

As a society, we're bent on self-preservation. It's all about me, me, me. Entitlement is the name of the game. But the gospel flips that script. Instead of self-preservation, it's self-sacrifice. Part of the problem is the belief that identity is there to be created when it's not. It's here to be discovered. The world says it's architecture – something we construct. The gospel says the opposite: it's archaeology – something we uncover that God's already given us. But if identity is there to be created, we foolishly think we're in charge of our lives, and anybody who says anything against us or what we want to do is the villain. But there's no guarantee that we can satisfactorily create this ideal life. And so, where's the hope in that? It might be exciting to think we can be whoever we want, but it doesn't take long to realise we can't. We need to align ourselves with God's plans.

Finding renewed purpose

Renewed purpose and seeing progress are what encourage us. Words of faith and support from others are precious, like, 'I can see how this will work.' We need that sort of community, don't we? I think having people around that you know you can trust is critical; getting closer to old friends is wise. People who know you're an idiot but don't care because they know that they're also idiots.

I lived off 2 Corinthians 4 for quite a while. I may feel crushed and abandoned, but Christianity is still true. So, whatever happens emotionally, I don't see a better story out there. You preach it to yourself first, like there is nowhere else to go if you want love to win and hope and joy to be real things. Apologetics became really important to me – not just a way to keep my head straight intellectually, but to remind me that since Christianity is actually true, there really is absolute meaning and purpose to pursue.

Ultimately, you have to believe that what God says about you is true, that the gospel is true. You do have to think that even though you're in the grave for much longer than you think is reasonable, there will be redemption and resurrection. Believing that God will turn the tide is so helpful. Believing that God sees and knows is helpful. Believing that there are still people you can count on is helpful. It's how you frame it in your mind. It's choosing not to let go of your faith. That's the big battle. Don't lose your faith. No storm lasts forever – really, even the British weather eventually changes. At some point, the clouds break. You've got to believe that God is for you because He really is.

Soaking in the Psalms

We must do something to get our encouraging sense of purpose and progress back. Do things that you enjoy. Tap into the things that remind you who you are and give you life. We must acknowledge our brokenness, but shouldn't sit in it for too long. Otherwise that's just victimhood. For me, it was starting to write and gig again. Purposeful activities like these also help us to see how we're moving forward.

The psalms are really helpful. I tend to have a psalm over each year. For this year, it's Psalm 42, 'Why, my soul, are you downcast?' It's brilliant, isn't it? The psalms acknowledge how terrible things are and then say, 'Come on, God. Well, You're not doing anything here.' And then they say, 'But I know that my God will do it.' They teach us to turn sadness and anger into something creative, which is another way of moving forward: purpose and progress again.

Scars convert people

We need to be reminded we're not going to win every battle. I've learned that the call to follow Jesus is sometimes a call to failure. It's not a call to worldly success. We will get knocked down, but ultimately we can get back up. Don't forget that what converted Thomas were Jesus' scars.[51] Whereas wounds can scare people, scars can convert them. So hold on. Because when storms pass and wounds heal, scars become powerful. We must work on our characters throughout for the healing to be complete. Don't take revenge, and don't badmouth people. Always be open for redemption, reconciliation, restoration, resurrection and revival. I find I'm carrying an authority now I never used to have because of what I've been through – scars convert people!

[51] John 20:24-28.

6

What have you forgotten?

If you've ever forgotten an important celebratory date, like someone close's birthday, you're not alone – I did, too. After eleven years of marriage, I let our anniversary slip. But, in a moment of fortunate marital coincidence, so did my wife. Why do we forget things that matter so much? Is it busyness? Distraction? Or something deeper?

Let's be honest: we rarely stop to think about our forgetfulness. It feels like one of those harmless things, doesn't it? Yet the Scriptures consistently emphasise its importance.

With the benefit of hindsight, I can see how forgetful I've been. As a church leader, I was too often looking forward, busily seeking to do the next best thing while neglecting to look back and give thanks. Busyness makes us blind, rushing makes us stop remembering and forgetfulness fuels discouragement.

I heard an outstanding West African Christian leader, facing the constant threat of persecution, challenge believers, saying that we forget we're the branch and neglect to allow God to be the vine.[52] It's why we're often

---

[52] Source not named to protect identity.

so dry. It's because we get so caught up in serving like Martha that we hardly make time to sit like Mary.[53] Mary Ministry appears unproductive, and even careless, but it is the one thing that Jesus said is necessary – to sit at His feet and receive.

One important way we can posture ourselves to receive is to remember. Ironically, however, we often forget the things God desires us to remember and remember what we're meant to forget (eg, our sins and Satan's lies). But when we fail to remember and reflect on 'noble', 'pure', 'lovely', 'admirable', 'excellent' and 'praiseworthy' things (Philippians 4:8), distorted ideas can creep in. Before long, we grow discouraged and mistakenly view God and others as uncaring, unkind or even malicious.

Remembering revisited

God's foundational calls to remembrance urge us to never lose sight of His unchanging, eternal nature, His mighty acts of deliverance and the holy rest He wants us to enjoy.

> God also said to Moses, 'Say this to the people of Israel: "The LORD [I AM WHO I AM], the God of your fathers, the God of Abraham, the God of Isaac, and the God of Jacob, has sent me to you." This is my name for ever, and thus I am to be remembered throughout all generations.'
> (Exodus 3:15, ESV; see also v 14)

Our God is entirely self-sufficient. He showed up as a self-nourished flame to Moses, independent of external fuel.

---

[53] See John 15:1-2; Luke 10:38-42.

He can create out of nothing – His power is awe-inspiring. He's also faithfully present through all generations, evidenced by the repetition of 'the God of' in the verse above. In our ever-changing, chaotic world, His unwavering good character is the constant we can rely on. He granted Abraham a child when it seemed impossible. He provided a substitute for Isaac so the blade didn't strike him. He shielded Jacob from his twin brother's vengeance.[54] Despite Abraham's wavering faith, Isaac's subsequent favouritism and Jacob's deceitful actions, God's faithfulness remained steadfast.

> Then Moses said to the people, 'Remember this day in which you came out from Egypt, out of the house of slavery, for by a strong hand the LORD brought you out from this place. No leavened bread shall be eaten.'
> (Exodus 13:3; ESV)

God was aware of the suffering His people endured in Egypt. He attentively listened to their cries and descended to liberate them from oppression through a sequence of ten extraordinary plagues. This culminated in the astonishing division of an entire sea. We're consistently encouraged to remember such mighty acts; Psalm 77 is a good example.

> Remember the Sabbath day, to keep it holy ... For in six days the LORD made heaven and earth, the sea, and all that is in them, and rested on the seventh

---

[54] See Genesis 21, 22, 32–33.

day. Therefore the LORD blessed the Sabbath day
and made it holy.
(Exodus 20:8, 11, ESV)

The Sabbath is an invitation to remember creation. Our
God, who 'will neither slumber nor sleep' (Psalm 121:4),
rested to bless us with a pattern for life. He invites us to
stop to consider His unparalleled creative ability – to be
reminded that He's more powerful than any opposition
we face.

Sabbath isn't just about recharging our spiritual
batteries. In Jewish thought, as explained by Abraham
Heschel, the first six days of creation are allegorically
paired, like mates – but the seventh day stands alone.
Because of this, the Sabbath is seen as the 'mate' of God's
people, a bit like Eve was to Adam.[55] In this sense, Sabbath
is an invitation to intimacy with God, to remember our
completeness in our relationship with Him, how our
brokenness has been supernaturally *kintsugi'd* through His
sublime sacrifice.

According to the second setting-out of the Ten
Commandments in Deuteronomy 5:12-15, it's also about
remembering we *were* slaves rescued by God. As John
Mark Comer put it, 'At Sinai it's a way of saying yes to God
and his world; in Deuteronomy it's a way of saying no to
Egypt and its system.'[56] We should remember we're

---

[55] Abraham Joshua Heschel, *The Sabbath*, New York: FSG
Classics, 2005, pp 51-55.
[56] John Mark Comer, *Garden City: Work, Rest, and the Art of Being
Human*, Grand Rapids, MI: Zondervan, 2015, p 205.

precious children of God, not insignificant machines in an oppressive regime.

Pause!

Which of God's original instructions to remember do you find yourself neglecting the most? How might this affect your understanding of His unchanging nature, mighty deliverance, or gift of holy rest? What transformation could regular, intentional remembering of these truths bring to your life?

Wrong remembering

It's not uncommon, however, for memories to get corrupted. The Israelites in the wilderness, for example, remembered 'the fish [they] ate in Egypt' (Numbers 11:4-6) but forgot Pharaoh's brutal baby killing as well as the floggings – the degrading and inhuman treatment they were rescued from. God had performed miracle after miracle to save them. He was now raining down manna from heaven. But their stomachs stopped them from rightly remembering, and they grumbled along with them.

It's possible for us to undermine our greater Exodus deliverance by failing to rightly remember the slavery-to-sin darkness we've been rescued from. But there's an important balance to be struck in such remembering, since God has repeatedly said He remembers our sins 'no more' (Isaiah 43:25; Jeremiah 31:34). What right do we have to disagree with God? 'If we confess our sins', the apostle John wrote, '[God] will forgive us our sins and purify us from all unrighteousness' (1 John 1:9). When we side with

God against our sins, He sends them away, He lifts them off, He covers them, He removes them, He blots them out, He tramples them underfoot, He casts them into the bottom of the ocean and He unremembers them.[57]

Another type of wrong remembering is when it's purely cerebral and not also sensory. In *Becoming Friends of Time*, John Swinton quotes the sociologist Rafael Narvaez, who points out that in Spanish, 'remember' means passing a moment of time back not only through the mind but also through the heart. It's meant, therefore, to be sensuous in nature, impacting the whole of who we are.[58]

> **Pause!**
>
> How might you balance rightly remembering the darkness of sin you've been rescued from with embracing God's forgiveness and unremembering of your sins? What would it look like for you to 'remember' God's grace not just intellectually but in a way that deeply impacts your heart and the whole of who you are?

David's remembering

When David encouraged himself in the Lord, what did he do? I'm confident he remembered God. When facing Goliath, he recalled how God protected him in the past:

---

[57] Leviticus 16:21-22; Psalm 32:1-2; Psalm 103:12; John 1:29; Isaiah 43:25; Isaiah 44:22; Micah 7:19; Jeremiah 31:34; Isaiah 43:25; Hebrews 8:12.

[58] John Swinton, *Becoming Friends of Time: Disability, Timefullness, and Gentle Discipleship*, London: SCM Press, 2021, p 150.

'The LORD who rescued me from the paw of the lion and the paw of the bear will rescue me from the hand of this Philistine' (1 Samuel 17:37). It fuelled his courage to confront the formidable and disheartening giant – despite being treated as insignificant by his father, called immoral by his brother and deemed incapable by his king. By remembering, David saw the Lord Almighty towering above this seemingly insurmountable human giant, and we can, too.

In 1 Samuel 30:1-6, David returned to his homestead which had been 'destroyed by fire', with all the women and children taken. His own men were talking of killing him. Why? Because he was guilty. He wasn't responsible for the Amalekite invasion, but was culpable for encouraging his men to become mercenaries for the Philistines, which poked the Amalekite bear to attack. It was undoubtedly a time of deep discouragement for David, as his sin, not just his unfortunate circumstances, bore down upon him. So what did he remember that awakened courage that could also make us brave? Answer: the grace of God.

Yes, David could have continued his lion-and-bear-remembering to include other victories God had granted him: from overcoming Goliath to when he saved the city of Keilah and found refuge in the 'Rock of Escape' (1 Samuel 23:28, ESV). These experiences would surely have remained etched on his memory, testifying to God's faithfulness. But I think David's remembering went deeper. I believe he remembered he was a nobody that no one noticed, forgotten even by his father – whom God took from the pasture to become a prince over His people. It was grace – the unmerited favour of God – that David would later give voice to with these words, 'Who am I, LORD God, and what is my family, that you have brought me this far?' (1 Chronicles 17:16).

In November 2022, I was honoured to represent the charity Open Doors at the inauguration of a prayer gathering for the reunification of North and South Korea. Standing before a room filled with remarkable saints – men and women who'd sacrificed so much for Christ's cause – I felt unworthy. There were many more qualified to speak, from the team I was part of to my interpreter who had been forced to leave China due to his brave missionary work. I spoke in front of a glass screen overlooking the border of North Korea, one of the most challenging countries in the world to be a Christian. If that wasn't humbling enough, our team was awarded The Order of Peace Korea Medal alongside prominent Koreans who'd dedicated decades to praying for reunification. This distinguished honour was crafted from the demilitarised zone's melted barbed wire and shell casings. I felt utterly undeserving.

This reminds me of the exuberant nature of God's grace – we're bestowed with spiritual blessings, like redemption and adoption, that we could never earn, as we read in Ephesians 1:3-8. But we shouldn't simply admire them, like medals displayed in cases. We must put them on, own them and live out their truth – that's how we show our gratitude for them.

I once asked a Muslim convert from Yemen, who regularly receives death threats, how he manages to overcome discouragement. He said:

Every morning, I lift my voice in praise because waking up as a Yemeni Christian is a miracle in itself. I praise the Lord Jesus Christ for His unfailing faithfulness, His salvation and His love that knows no end. He is my God, my Saviour, my everything. My heart rejoices in Him, and I surrender each day to His purpose, asking Him to use me for the glory of His Kingdom. Every single day is a testimony of His love![59]

David's remembering was reinforced by godly friendships. Jonathan came to his aid during the exhausting period when David fled from Saul and his army. He helped David 'find strength' and encouragement in God (1 Samuel 23:15-18).[60] Jonathan reassured David that he would become Israel's king (as God had promised through Samuel). I can almost envision Jonathan emphatically urging David to believe in this, saying, 'Trust it wholeheartedly, because I do!'

The Holy Spirit is our true and better Jonathan, the unrivalled encourager who reminds us of all that God has said.[61] The Spirit 'testifies with our spirit that we are God's children' (Romans 8:16). Our remembering, then, isn't all about self-effort but asking for help from the Holy Spirit!

Pause!
Who are the 'Jonathans' in your life, the friends who remind you of God's goodness?

---

[59] Used with permission.
[60] Note: the same word for encouragement/strength as used in 1 Samuel 30:6 is used here.
[61] John 14:26.

How could you start and/or strengthen that relationship? And who might need your encouragement? Friends come in all forms – counsellors, spiritual directors and believers whose testimonies lift our spirits. If God has worked in their lives, He can do it in ours. Who might *your* story spark hope in?

Remembering restored

The New Testament picks up where the Old left off, with its authors repeatedly saying it's no trouble for them to remind us about the same gospel truths.[62] The most important exhortation, of course, came from Jesus Himself: 'do this in remembrance of me' (Luke 22:19). Through this memorial meal, God provides a way for us to remember and experience His profound love, figuratively feasting on His broken body and tasting His shed blood. We remember *the* demonstration of God's love – dying to deliver us from the death we deserve – as we symbolically re-enact it.

In addition to taking communion, reading Scripture, singing worship songs and paying attention to good Bible teaching, here are some other ways we can keep God's truth fresh in our minds.

Objects

In Numbers 15:37-41, the Israelites were told to attach tassels with a blue cord to their clothing, reminding them to follow God's commands and live set apart. What simple objects or symbols could help you remember who you are in Christ?

---

[62] 1 Corinthians 15:1; Philippians 3:1; 2 Peter 1:12.

Festivals

The seven Jewish festivals reconnected God's people to their origins (Genesis) and journey (Exodus). Today, we celebrate Lent, Easter, Advent and Christmas and have gatherings such as Big Church Festival, Connect Festival, Creation Fest, David's Tent, Focus, Keswick, More Together, New Wine, Spring Harvest and Wildfires. They can help us remember who God is, rediscover our purpose and encounter His presence together.

Places

Just as Joshua on behalf of the Israelites 'set up ... twelve stones' to commemorate their miraculous crossing of the Jordan (Joshua 4:9), significant places in Christian history can inspire hope within us as we reflect on God's works there in times past. There came a time when Brother Andrew, the young Dutchman who was inspired to smuggle Bibles into Communist Eastern Europe, was discouraged.[63] He desperately wanted to get to Bulgaria, but Yugoslavian officials forced him to take the long way round, a 1,500-mile detour. He described an intense depression settling over him. He was going to miss his wife's birthday. He might not even get back in time for the birth of his child. He was literally bent double with back pain from driving massive distances. Discouragement was working its poison in him when he saw a road sign that looked familiar. He stopped the car. It was Philippi, where Paul and Silas had miraculously escaped from prison. As

---

[63] Brother Andrew, *God's Smuggler: One Man's Mission to Change the World*, 60th Anniversary Edition, London: Hodder, 2015, pp 167-169.

he soaked in the historic ambience of that holy place, the chains of depression that had oppressed him were broken, just as they had on the apostles' wrists in Acts 16:26. Not only did heaviness leave, but he realised he was also standing upright, without pain. He ran back to the car with joy, setting off again to encourage more persecuted believers. It's amazing what remembering can do!

Stop and think

- What are the things God most wants you to remember, and how can you be intentional about focusing on them rather than the lies and distractions that lead us away from Him?

- Imagine what it could be like for you to embrace a regular Sabbath – a sacred space for rest, worship and restoration. How could you intentionally set aside this time? When might you do it? Who could encourage or join you in this practice?

- What would it look like, and what might the impact be, for you to begin each day by putting on the spiritual blessings God has given us? Are there any daily declarations you could start your day with that might help?

- What festival(s) could you attend or places could you visit to remember God's faithfulness?

7

Godly faith over ungodly fear
Esha*

Name changed for security reasons.

Expecting resistance

The first time my husband was threatened for his faith, we knew our journey with Jesus would not be easy. In Bangladesh, a Muslim country where Christians are a tiny minority, following Christ often comes at a high cost. I was born into a Christian family, but my husband grew up in a devout Muslim home. His father, an esteemed imam, expected him to carry on the family's legacy. But God had other plans.

One day, my husband received a small booklet about Jesus. Out of curiosity, he read it. That curiosity turned into deeper searching. He was given a New Testament pocket Bible that he secretly began to read. He fell in love with Jesus, especially when he encountered the verse, 'Jesus answered, "I am the way and the truth and the life. No one comes to the Father except through me"' (John 14:6). Despite knowing what it might cost him, he chose to follow Christ.

From that moment, life became very difficult. His family rejected him. His community turned against him. He lost everything he had known. I have learned that when we truly follow Jesus, resistance will come. There is a lie that says if we follow Jesus, life will be easy. But the truth is, the closer we walk with Him, the more we will face resistance. It's because when God moves, the enemy fights back. I've seen this firsthand. But I've also seen that no matter how intense the battle, Jesus is always greater.

Holding on to my identity

The persecution my husband faced was severe. His family could not accept that one of their own had chosen Christianity. They tried everything – threatening him, even arranging a marriage for him to a Muslim woman to force him back into Islam. But my husband refused to deny Jesus.

When he asked me to marry him, I knew it would not be easy. In our culture, marriage is not a personal decision – it involves the entire family. Both our families opposed our union. My parents feared what could happen to us, and his family were outraged.

We, however, knew God was calling us to be together. But after we were married, his family declared him dead. They wanted nothing to do with him. That, however, wasn't enough. One night they came for him. A mob of more than a hundred men dragged him away. They beat him brutally, intending to kill him. Their plan was to hang his decapitated head in the marketplace in the village as a warning to others.

I will never forget that night. I was at my parents' home, unaware of what was happening. In the early hours of the morning, a man from the village came running to our house, shouting, 'Your husband is dead! They're coming for you next!'

I wanted to run to where my husband was, to hold him. But my family forced me to flee. I prayed, 'Lord, I want to see him once more. No matter how, if alive or whatever way you want me to meet, I want to see him.'

I left my home with a broken heart. For two days I lived in grief, believing my husband was gone. But on the third day, God did the impossible. My husband returned. God is mighty to save. He still does miracles today. My husband was wounded and in physical pain, but he was alive.

God had made a way for him to escape. Some of the Muslim people who accompanied the rickshaw pullers, transporting him to where he was potentially to be killed, realised he was not going to deny his faith. God miraculously worked in their hearts and, instead of taking him to his execution, they helped him to flee. God can even turn enemies into friends.

That night, I realised something profound: my identity is not in my circumstances. It is not in the approval of my family or my community. It is in Christ alone. The fear of death was so real, but God healed me and it no longer rules in my heart.

The truth of Romans 14:8 – 'If we live, we live for the Lord; and if we die, we die for the Lord. So, whether we live or die, we belong to the Lord' – became our family verse and has carried us through every trial since. It teaches us to live with godly faith, not ungodly fear. So, whatever discouragement you're facing, remember this: you belong to Jesus and nothing can take that away from you. They can torture us and kill our bodies, but not our souls, which are already secured in the Lord. And what's amazing is that our story isn't unique in South East Asia. The Church is growing despite strong opposition. Men, women and children are coming to Jesus and experiencing assurance of salvation because they find the word of God is powerful, as they are carried along by the prayers of the righteous.

Trusting in God

For years, my husband and I lived with uncertainty. We had no permanent home. We faced continued threats. We had to start over with nothing. But through it all, we saw God's hand at work. He provided. He protected. He guided us step by step. Discouragement often comes when we feel like God is not moving fast enough. But I have learned that His timing is always perfect.

Today, my husband and I serve the persecuted Church in South East Asia. We walk alongside others who, like us, have suffered for their faith. We encourage them, pray with them and remind them that they are not alone.

We could have chosen bitterness. We could have let discouragement define us. But instead, we let God use our pain for His glory. Discouragement will come. Resistance will come. But our hope is greater than our hardship.

8
To what extent are you enquiring?

Chances are, you've come across movies with lacklustre storylines, but there's a particular film that may have escaped your radar: *Ballistic*.[64] And there's a compelling reason for its obscurity. It's been called the worst movie ever made. Critics condemned it: 'a startlingly inept film … overblown, wall-to-wall action without a hint of wit, coherence, style, or originality.'[65] Its $70 million production budget, famous actors and many special effects failed to salvage its flawed narrative. It teaches us a profoundly important life lesson: no amount of superficial glitz and glamour can rescue an unsatisfying story. What we need is an entirely new script.

Frequently, the narrative that guides our lives can be one we've created ourselves. But if we're honest, most of us lack the experience and wisdom to craft a truly remarkable story. I mean, do we always know what's best for us?

---

[64] 2002; distributed by Warner Bros, Warner Bros Pictures, UFA GmbH.

[65] 'Ballistic: Ecks vs Sever', *Rotten Tomatoes*, www.rottentomatoes.com/m/ballistic_ecks_vs_sever (accessed 12th December 2024).

I love how Edith Nesbit expressed it in *The Railway Children*. If you don't know the story, a family mysteriously lost their dad and were forced to downsize and move to the country. The children don't know why. Only their mother knows the terrible truth at this point, that their daddy is in prison, falsely convicted of treason. Peter, the son, asks his mother, who's been working as a part-time writer to try to make ends meet, if she'd prefer to write a book making their dad return quickly because he missed him terribly. All of a sudden, Peter's mother puts her arms around him and holds him for a full sixty seconds. Isn't that how God might sometimes want to minister to us? A majestic embrace of all the marvellous maternal qualities of His love?[66]

Then, with quiet conviction, she speaks. Life, she says, isn't just unfolding randomly – it is part of a greater story, carefully crafted by hands far wiser than her own. If she were the one shaping the narrative she might get things wrong. But God knows exactly how to bring everything together for the best possible ending. Peter asks if she really believes that. Most of the time, yes, she explains. But there are moments when her certainty falters. Even then she tries to cling to the truth, despite her heart struggling to feel it.[67]

---

[66] See Deuteronomy 32:11; Psalm 71:6; Isaiah 49:15; 66:13; Luke 13:34.

[67] Edith Nesbit, *The Railway Children* (1906), chapter 13, www.gutenberg.org/files/1874/1874-h/1874-h.htm (accessed 12th December 2024).

This beautifully echoes one of the Bible's more neglected but perhaps most powerful prayers, 'I do believe; help me overcome my unbelief!' (Mark 9:24).

'My Way', thanks to Frank Sinatra's soulful rendition, remains not just one of the most popular songs people want to have played at their funeral but also the soundtrack to their life. It's hard not to tune into it, to be honest, because it's being broadcast to us all the time. But what if 'my way' is a poorly written script?

Pause!

In what ways has the 'My Way' narrative shaped your decisions or perspective? How might this have influenced the course of your story?

Catastrophe

Several chapters of David's will being done resulted in catastrophe. He did not enquire of the Lord before vengefully going after Nabal. He did not seek the Father's will before marrying Abigail and slipping further down the patriarchal slope of polygamy and dysfunctional family life that would give birth to mutiny.[68] He did not ask for God's guidance before deciding to serve Israel's enemies as a duplicitous trigger man.[69]

In 1 Samuel 30, however, after preaching to himself, David began praying to God again: 'and David enquired of the LORD' (1 Samuel 30:8). David did what Jesus urged His followers to do, 'seek first' the kingdom of God (Matthew 6:33) by praying 'your kingdom come, your will

---

[68] 1 Samuel 25.
[69] 1 Samuel 27.

be done' (Matthew 6:10, emphasis mine). It's what Jesus majestically modelled, under intense pressure in the Garden of Gethsemane, praying to the point of sweating blood, 'yet not my will, but *yours* be done' (Luke 22:42, emphasis mine).

When David enquired and obeyed, things went well, and when he didn't and lived life his own way, they didn't. Bringing the Ark of the Covenant back to Jerusalem is another example, as we see in 2 Samuel 6. He assumed the best way was the pragmatically convenient cart and oxen method (used by the Philistines – see 1 Samuel 6:7-9). This worldly wisdom cost a man his life. They disastrously overestimated their own holiness and desperately underestimated God's. 'We did not enquire of him,' David said, 'about how to do it in the prescribed way' (1 Chronicles 15:13). It should have been carried with poles on the shoulders of consecrated Levites – with reverent awe for the presence of God. When they walked the way of the Ark and not the cart, a tidal wave of joy had David dancing in his undergarments on the grave of discouragement.[70]

Pause!

Looking back, can you identify a moment when you chose the way of the cart over the way of the Ark? What was the outcome, and what lessons did you draw from that experience?

Having seen how straying from God's will can lead to discouragement and even disaster, it's clear that aligning

---

[70] 2 Samuel 6:14.

ourselves with His guidance isn't just important; it's essential. This naturally raises two key questions: how do we seek His direction and how can we truly discern His voice amid the noise of life?

How do we enquire?

Courageously, taking a deep breath and trusting God, no matter the cost. Let's try to imagine together what would have happened if God had said, 'Don't go after the Amalekites,' to David. His fighting men would not have been pleased – an understatement. But David asked God and didn't assume he knew best, even if that could mean death. Our approach to seeking God's guidance should go beyond merely wanting to understand His will. It should have within it the courage to act upon it, even if it leads to becoming unpopular.

How do we hear God?

A lot could be said here. There are so many ways God speaks. Personal experience, however, has taught me that the most crucial aspect is cultivating a state of stillness so we can recognise God's presence: in the Bible verses we read, in the faithful Christians we talk to and in the awe-inspiring beauty of creation. Christ is present, though often in a hidden way, much like He was with the discouraged disciples on the road to Emmaus, revealing Himself with patient timing and tender compassion. This means that our scepticism can decrease and our curiosity should increase. God is present! As Psalm 139 teaches, there's nowhere we can go from His presence. Jesus promised to be with us '*always*, to the very end of the age'

(Matthew 28:20, emphasis mine). We must look for His encouraging presence!

Years ago, my name was unexpectedly nominated for an internship at a US law firm specialising in death penalty defence work. At that time, I was practising as a fledgling barrister, and accepting this opportunity would likely mean a career change. Throughout this decision-making process, I turned to my Bible for guidance. I chatted with experienced Christians and sought divine direction, asking God if I should embark on this new path. About a week later, in a meeting, my attention was inexplicably drawn to some unusual wording on the spine of a book on a nearby bookshelf. After the gathering, I felt compelled to open it. The words 'Kansas City, Missouri' were written inside. It struck me as a sign because this was the location of the law firm. So I decided to take a leap of faith and accept the opportunity. The experience was positively life-changing. I couldn't have scripted this unexpected turn of events myself, but it became clear that God had a better plan in mind. Remarkable doors for sharing my faith opened up. I enjoyed rich, Spirit-led worship and heard foundation-laying teachings about developing intimacy with God at the church I attended. And before the internship finished, God provided a great new job to get into back in the UK.

We should be discerning when it comes to circumstantial experiences, however, being careful not to give spiritual weight to things that merely confirm our own preferences, not God's. Think of Jonah. He didn't want to preach to the ungodly Ninevites, so he went to the nearest ferry terminal to head in the opposite direction. It just so happened a boat was right there, ready to take him far away from Nineveh to a holiday destination. 'God must want me to get on board,' he could have reasoned. 'Why else would He have provided this ship?' But God had already spoken, 'Arise, go to Nineveh' (Jonah 1:2, ESV) – not Tarshish! It's a storm warning tale about aligning our decisions with God's Word.

God's will is 'good, pleasing and perfect' (Romans 12:2), but it's not always pleasureful or peaceful. The persecuted Church reminds us, along with Scripture, that 'in this world [we] will have trouble' (John 16:33). So, in our relatively pampered context, it's important to know that feeling peace about something isn't necessarily the best guide to having found God's will. We may actually feel disturbed, or feel nothing at all.

The way not to be deceived, particularly by subjective feelings, is to ensure our minds are regularly renewed. It's what Romans 12:1-2 teaches:

> Therefore, I urge you, brothers and sisters, in view of God's mercy, to offer your bodies as a living sacrifice, holy and pleasing to God – this is your true and proper worship. Do not conform to the pattern of this world, but be transformed by the renewing of your mind. Then you will be able to test and approve what God's will is – his good, pleasing and perfect will.

Commenting on these verses, the Chinese preacher Brother Yun said that our heavenly Father wants us to put Jesus at the centre of our lives so we can discern His will by putting our own plans away. He wrote, 'We must bundle up all our hopes, dreams and future plans and lay them at the feet of Jesus.'[71] Despite enduring brutal beatings, imprisonment and persecution, he assures us that Jesus is much better at running our lives than we are, and the story He writes for us is always richer and more beautiful than anything we could write for ourselves.

Stop and think

- How often do you pause to enquire of God before making significant decisions, and how could this practice increase your trust in His plan?

- Are there areas of your life where you need to let go of control and trust that God's script for you is better than your own? What holds you back from doing so?

- Reflecting on times when you've sought God's guidance, in what ways have you acted with the courage to follow His will, even when it seemed unpopular or challenging?

---

[71] Brother Yun, *Living Water : Powerful Teachings from the International Bestselling Author of* The Heavenly Man, Grand Rapids, MI: Zondervan, 2008, p 93.

9
Begin with beloved
Rachael Newham

Rachael is a theology of mental health specialist, speaker and writer. She served as the Mental Health Friendly Church project manager at Kintsugi Hope and founded the mental health charity ThinkTwice. She spends much of her time travelling the country preaching, speaking and writing about issues related to faith and mental health. She's the author of Learning to Breathe *(London: SPCK, 2018) and* And Yet *(London: Form, 2021), in which she delves deeply into the interplay of joy and lament. Her latest book is* Beloved is Where We Begin *(London: Form, 2025). For more information, visit rachaelnewham.com*

Discouragement says, 'You can't do that'

Whereas encouragement gives you courage, confidence and some sense of power, discouragement does the opposite. It's the language of, 'You can't do that; you shouldn't do that... this is the person you're never going to be.' It's a strange mixture of not just the disappointment we might feel about ourselves, but also hopelessness that comes from all directions, including concerns about the state of the world.

My discouragement, though, mainly comes from myself. Everybody around me is usually hugely encouraging, from family to work colleagues. It's my inner critic's constant disparaging voice, part and parcel of mental illness, that's my biggest discouragement. It's the thing saying, 'You're never going to be able to do that.'

Accept limits; reject lies

One of the most discouraging parts of being really ill was the persistent belief this was as good as it would get. Discouragement is so often a lack of hope. When you're discouraged, hope requires bravery to say things can get better. So if you're at the point where you're so discouraged you don't believe that's possible, then hope doesn't feel possible either.

For me, a big part of the battle is working out what's true and what isn't. Aspects of my life are limited because of mental illness. I know, for example, that I can't work a full-time, traditional nine-to-five job. I've attempted it every few years, and it hasn't gone well. So there's a sense of realising this is something I must accept.

Limits don't necessarily need to be discouragements, though. Sometimes they can become encouragements that say, 'Here is what you can do.' Whether you have a mental illness or not, we all have limits of various kinds, and working within and accepting them is a way we can flourish. But it's those discouragements that claim we can't do *anything* worthwhile that aren't true. In the midst of mental illness, working out what's discouragement and what's a limit that I need to accept is really difficult. Mental illness muddies the waters of what can and can't be trusted.

Get stuff out of your head and into the world

I've found my spiritual life pretty dry in such times. The best thing I've done is keep an open communication line with God through writing. My diary reads a lot like a lament. It's Psalm 88-like: 'Where are you? What are you doing, God? I can't see you moving. I can't see you working.' I've never lost faith that God is real, but I have perhaps lost faith in His character.

There's something in journalling that encourages me. I expect if we could ask the psalmists and writers of laments, they'd tell us it's empowering to get stuff out of your head and into the world, whether talking, writing or painting. By doing so, we're inviting the possibility of hope. God, of course, already knows what we're going through, but if we don't externalise our experience in some way, we don't properly engage with Him. I love the Scripture that says God stands at the door and knocks.[72] He doesn't swoop in without us inviting Him.

Embracing the grind

I grew up in the nineties when it was all about dramatic testimonies and big expressions of God's presence in the Church. Only now I find myself identifying with the discouragement of the often-forgotten elder brother of prodigal son parable fame. When you've been slogging along, not doing anything drastic, just keeping going, you begin to wonder whether God sees you and whether He's with you in the same way as He seems with those having a mountaintop-type experience of Him running and hugging them.

---

[72] Revelation 3:20.

Life is so often a grind, but that doesn't mean it's not also a joy. Like any relationship, it's both. So I think it can be helpful to be slightly petulant with God sometimes, through the trials and the tedium, knowing that actually, He's OK with that. My child is the most petulant towards my husband and me. He'll say stuff to us he'd never say at preschool because he trusts that we'll always be there. The same is true of God. God says it's OK to beat our fists on His chest. There are consequences if we do stuff out of that anger, frustration and disappointment, but the point isn't that He'll change things because of it – it's that we're free to get it off our chest and be honest with Him.

Find safe spaces

When we're discouraged, we need safe spaces to honestly answer the question, 'How are you doing?' Kintsugi Hope runs wellbeing groups covering a range of topics over twelve weeks that help with this. They're great places to say what we need to say about what hurts. Sharing that you're not OK is a critical step to recovering hope. It doesn't mean we always tell everyone, but with trusted people in safe settings we should, because it permits others to do the same. We must work to create a Christian culture that doesn't expect us to always be shiny, happy people.

Good news vs happy news

Somewhere along the line, we got confused with the fact that Christianity is good news, whereas we've kind of thought of it as happy news, but actually, it isn't always happy. Jesus said we 'will have trouble' (John 16:33). He 'wept' (John 11:35). He died on a cross that wasn't happy or shiny. Sometimes, there's a real temptation that our churches must be places where we're always happy, and negative feelings aren't allowed because that won't attract unbelievers. This approach may get people through the door, but it's not how people will stay. Why? Because it's not discipleship. Discipleship is about learning to hold two truths together: that life is hard, but God is good, and it's the most uncomfortable tension – that's why we need the bridge of lament.

Lament is...

Lament is not just moaning; let's face it, Christians and people in general are good at moaning. We know how to do that. But lament is more than that; it's expressing the moan, if you like, with the expectation that God will do something with it. Like the patriarch Jacob, it's about wrestling our thoughts, emotions, and assumptions into alignment with who God is.[73]

Very few of us would admit we hold to a prosperity gospel, right? And yet, we kind of all do. We think almost subconsciously that if we tithe regularly, we'll be entitled to a measure of financial security; if we raise our kids right, they'll follow Jesus. We think we'll get something in return if we just do the right stuff. But that's not the gospel. The gospel is to put everything down and come and follow Jesus. It won't be easy, but isn't that the way of the cross? At the same time, though, it's the road to glory. So much of faith, I think, is holding two completely contradictory things together, quite often in a painful way. The goodness of God, the pain of life, the utter humiliation of the cross with the glory of heaven, knowing that the cross beat death, but actually it still hurt.

---

[73] Genesis 32:22-32.

Following the COVID-19 lockdowns, I noticed several church sermon series on Nehemiah – a reflection of the understandable desire to talk about rebuilding, as 'the joy of the LORD is [our] strength' (Nehemiah 8:10). But so often, what's neglected in the story is that Nehemiah wept over the walls of a city he'd not even visited for four months. I'm concerned that we should put in the work of grieving before we launch into the excitement of something new. As Barbara Brown Taylor beautifully said about new life, 'Whether it is a seed in the ground, a baby in the womb, or Jesus in the tomb, it starts in the dark.'[74] But because of the way we've structured church and life, we rarely spend enough time in the dark to let stuff grow.

Wrestling in the dark

This wrestling in the dark is uncomfortable. It's not where we want to be. But it's so vital. For example, I think we're missing something significant at Easter if we don't connect with the rawness of the disciples' grief, who didn't know for sure Resurrection Sunday was coming.

I think other cultures have so much to teach us about grieving and sitting with discouragement. In the case of bereavement, the Jews *shiva* for seven days, where they just grieve, and then there's another thirty-day period, and if you're a widow you wear black for a year.

We must allow ourselves and the people in our churches to grieve. Too often, we use 1 Thessalonians 4:13 as a prescription against grieving, but it doesn't say we should not grieve. It encourages us not to grieve as those without hope. So Christians are meant to grieve, just differently.

---

[74] Barbara Brown Taylor, *Learning to Walk in the Dark,* San Francisco, CA: HarperOne, 2014, p 122.

Opening up ways of doing that, whether it's a bereavement service or Blue Christmas event, or holding a prayer service on Holy Saturday when you wait between the cross and the resurrection, are not necessarily easy, but they're good starting points to help us process grief in a godly way.

Comfortably uncomfortable

We have to get comfortable with being uncomfortable. We have to get a sense that we won't always be happy. Jesus wasn't always happy, so why on earth would we expect to be? But Jesus was connected to the Father in prayer; see, for example, His deep wrestling with the Father in the Garden of Gethsemane, praying, 'May this cup be taken from me' (Matthew 26:39). We need to be able to grieve our losses and accept our limits and yet praise God through it, sometimes with tears and sometimes with clapping and dancing – but actually, they're all valid.

Follow the liturgical year

Following the liturgical year has been so helpful for me, having not grown up with that tradition. There's so much richness in having set seasons for life. That doesn't mean our emotions will always align with them. We're not always going to be waiting for something in Advent. We're not always going to be hoping and rejoicing at Easter. But there's something important about practising how to grieve, repent, wait and rejoice together so that, when we come up against them for real, we know the language to use. When we've done it as a community, we then know how to support one another through the different seasons when they come as well.

If you're new to liturgy, the *Book of Common Prayer* is a great place to start, alongside theologian Fleming Rutledge's devotional, *Means of Grace*.[75]

Beloved is where we begin

The phrase that's followed me around for the last year or so is that 'beloved is where we begin'. We don't begin in our despair. That's not where it started. Jesus' ministry began with the Spirit saying, 'This is my Son, whom I love; with him I am well pleased' (Matthew 3:17). I was part of a discussion panel at a national conference in 2023, and one of the questions was, 'How do we start the Christian story without talking about the Fall?' I said we start with the fact that we're called 'very good' (Genesis 1:31). We hold on to this truth that we, as believers, are beloved through it all, through the lows and highs. I think this is the greatest hope and encouragement.

---

[75] Fleming Rutledge, *Means of Grace: A Year of Weekly Devotions*, Grand Rapids, MI: William B Eerdmans Publishing, 2021.

10
How are your neighbours?

We've probably all heard the phrase, 'Put your own oxygen mask on first' – maybe during a pre-flight safety briefing or a leadership seminar. The idea is that we can't effectively help others if we're not OK. It's a reminder of the importance of self-care, and it's absolutely valid. But here's the thing – if we're not careful, self-care can slip into self-absorption. Instead of just securing our own oxygen mask first, metaphorically we might also put our chairs into the upright position, organise our belongings, check our seatbelt and scroll through our phones – all the while forgetting others around us may be struggling to breathe.

In such self-absorption, we can miss out on the life-giving mission of God. We can forfeit the dignified sense of purpose that derives from acts of service and stop flourishing in the way God intended. Jesus said, 'It is more *blessed* to give than to receive' (Acts 20:35, emphasis mine). 'Blessed' means flourishing. It's a principle woven throughout Scripture, exemplified in passages like Isaiah 58:10-11:

> If you spend yourselves on behalf of the hungry
> and satisfy the needs of the oppressed,

then your light will rise in the darkness,
and your night will become like the noonday.
The LORD will guide you always;
he will satisfy your needs in a sun-scorched land
and will strengthen your frame.
You will be like a well-watered garden,
like a spring whose waters never fail.

To truly detox discouragement, we must find encouragement from doing 'good works, which God prepared in advance for us to do' (Ephesians 2:10). This is how we can resist finding identity in victimhood and root it in Christ instead. We live, as American psychologists Jean Twenge and Keith Campbell put it, in a narcissism epidemic, a time of entitlement.[76] Let's not conform to the spirit of the age but rightly respond to the call of God, who invites each of us, in accordance with our unique stories and particular giftings, to comfort others with the comfort we have received from Him, turning evil for good.[77]

The shift from healthy self-care to unhealthy self-focus is something we need to watch out for, particularly when life feels hard and we're tempted to retreat inward. But what if, in tough times, lifting our gaze to notice and help others is actually part of God's plan for our own healing?

That's what we see in 1 Samuel 30. David had every reason to be discouraged. But as he set out in obedience to God's leading, something unexpected happened. He and his men came across a man from Egypt, the nation that

[76] Jean M Twenge and W Keith Campbell, *The Narcissism Epidemic: Living in the Age of Entitlement*, New York: Atria Books, 2010.
[77] 2 Corinthians 1:4.

infamously oppressed Israel. This Egyptian was an Amalekite slave who'd been callously cast aside and left for dead simply because he'd fallen ill; to them, he was worthless. If there was ever someone David could justify walking past, it was this man, especially as he could've been directly involved in the attack on their home. But in a fascinating prefiguring of the parable of the Good Samaritan in Luke 10:25-37, David's company showed compassion. They stopped. They gave him food to eat and water to drink and took care of him.

It's striking that David and his men didn't bargain with the man, or make their compassion conditional on the promise of useful information. Instead, they displayed countercultural kindness, and something remarkable happened: 'his spirit revived' (1 Samuel 30:12, ESV). The man who had been discarded became the very guide God used to reveal the next step in their rescue mission. A vulnerable stranger, once overlooked and forgotten, became a key player in God's redemptive plan.

Pause!

How can we distinguish between healthy self-care and unhealthy self-focus in our daily lives? What could we do to ensure that our care for ourselves equips us to better serve others, rather than retreat inward? How might the principle of 'spend[ing] yourselves on behalf of the hungry' (Isaiah 58:10) guide your approach to balancing these dynamics?

Who?

'Go and do likewise', Jesus said to His self-justifying questioner (Luke 10:37). Be like the Good Samaritan. Neighbours include our perceived enemies. They are image bearers in need, regardless of our feelings towards them. We must continually view *all* people as God does – the precious pinnacle of His creation.

Ping An, a Chinese landscape painter in Shanghai, underwent a profound transformation when she came to faith. She was studying traditional Chinese landscape art, in which people are typically depicted in miniature. They're deliberately overshadowed by the grandeur of nature. She, however, was inspired by Genesis 1 and started drawing landscapes with human figures as the central focus. This unconventional approach drew the attention of her supervisors. They angrily questioned her. They argued that we humans are insignificant because we're here for such a short time compared to immovable mountains.

With great courage, Ping An quoted Luke 21:33: 'Heaven and earth will pass away, but my words will never pass away.' It's God's words, she told them, that make things significant: 'He doesn't talk to the mountains. He talks to us. He made the mountains for us! Isn't it incredible?'[78] She was expelled from her university and now works as a teacher, painting portraits in her spare time. But what she said was 'very good' (Genesis 1:31).

---

[78] Ron Boyd-MacMillan, *Faith That Endures: The Essential Guide to the Persecuted Church*, Lancaster: Sovereign World Limited, 2006, p 324.

How?

This parable of the Good Samaritan is not only about who is a neighbour, but also about how we extend kindness. Given the historical context, we might even have expected the Samaritan to further harm the injured Jewish man. His response, however, is marked by profound compassion. He stops, placing himself at risk since robbers could still be nearby. He willingly shares his resources and provides immediate first aid. Then he lifts the injured man onto his donkey and takes him to an inn which, given the absence of such establishments in the vicinity, must have been in Jewish Jericho. Middle Eastern Bible scholar Ken Bailey says it would have been like a Native American walking into Dodge City with a scalped cowboy on his horse. Even though he'd saved the cowboy's life, he'd be lucky to get out alive.[79] The courage displayed is remarkable. It points to the selfless, sacrificial, extra-mile love Jesus spoke of in Matthew 5:41. It's the cross-shaped love He demonstrated, willingly paying the ultimate price for our sins to heal our brokenness and bring us back to life.

Discouragement, however, has a way of pulling us in the opposite direction. It casts our eyes downward and inward, trapping us in cycles of self-pity and procrastination. It's this miserable mindset that can cause us to miss out on the next step of our restorative journey with Jesus. So, from the cross, Jesus calls us to something greater. He lifts our gaze. He draws us out of ourselves. He points us to the liberating *other*-centred love that now,

[79] Kenneth Bailey, *Poet & Peasant and Through Peasant Eyes: A Literary-Cultural Approach to the Parables in Luke*, Grand Rapids, MI: William B Eerdmans Publishing, 1983, p 575.

by grace, envelops us. The love that declared 'Father, forgive them' (Luke 23:34), despite the agonies of crucifixion. The love that saw even His mockers and enemies who put Him there as worth dying for.

Where?

So where do we start? For me, it began with the people closest to me – the ones I feared I'd neglected in my own struggle with discouragement. I asked God for wisdom and started with simple questions like, 'How is my wife?' and 'How are my children?' I kept trying, even when my expressions of love felt modest. Little by little, I saw how these small acts of care made a difference. From there, my circle has slowly grown.

There are so many neighbours in need, from traumatised refugees to quiet co-workers struggling with their mental health. They might even be someone you see every day but haven't really *noticed* in a while.

The beloved St Francis of Assisi, known for his profound servitude, experienced a period of genuine doubt about whether God truly cared for him. God responded to his questioning through a vision. St Francis saw Christ Himself, His gaze fixed upon him from the cross, radiating such a profound love that it melted his soul and dissipated all discouragement. May the prayer he has become renowned for (although probably not penned by him) help us all surrender to God's will as we seek to serve others without neglecting our self-care:

> Lord, make me an instrument of your peace:
> where there is hatred, let me sow love;
> where there is injury, pardon;

where there is doubt, faith;
where there is despair, hope;
where there is darkness, light;
where there is sadness, joy.
O divine Master, grant that I may not so much seek
to be consoled as to console,
to be understood as to understand,
to be loved as to love.
For it is in giving that we receive,
it is in pardoning that we are pardoned,
and it is in dying that we are born to eternal life.
Amen.[80]

Stop and think

- In what ways could lifting your gaze to notice and help others contribute to your own healing and spiritual growth, as well as that of others?

- Who are the 'Egyptians' God would like you to serve? Look around and ask yourself, 'How are they?'

- How can the Scriptures and Ping An's insights help you see the people around you as the precious pinnacle of God's creation?

---

[80] Unknown author, 'Peace Prayer', Loyola Press, www.loyolapress.com/catholic-resources/prayer/traditional-catholic-prayers/saints-prayers/peace-prayer-of-saint-francis (accessed 14th February 2025). Although often attributed to St Francis of Assisi, this prayer probably originated in the early twentieth century.

11

Sanctify success
Tola Doll Fisher

Tola is the creative director and editor of the Premier Woman Alive *brand and writes as an opinion columnist on topics including sex and relationships, baby loss, wellbeing and success. She's delivered a TEDx Talk called 'Debunking the Myth of Success' and was listed as one of* The Voice *newspaper's women to watch for its International Women's Day special in 2018. She's the co-host of* Sisterhood on TBN UK *and author of the encouraging book* Still Standing: 100 Lessons from an 'Unsuccessful' Life' *(London: SPCK, 2020). She writes on life lessons based on the themes in her book here: stillstanding.substack.com*

A persistent feeling of hopelessness

Discouragement, for me, is a persistent feeling of hopelessness, the compounded sense that stuff just isn't working out the way we want it to. I'm divorced, and just before that, we had a daughter, Annie, who died not long after birth. People said, 'Don't worry, you'll get pregnant again.' Another even predicted, 'You're going to have twins.' That was more than a decade ago, and I haven't been pregnant since. Even with my husband, I had people saying things like, 'You guys will get back together again.' But he got remarried, and I got cancer.

Whether your challenge is heartbreak, career disappointment or chronic illness, the principle remains: God's presence and goodness are not measured by our life's immediate outcomes.

Let down by God

In tough times, though, it seems as if God has completely let us down. It's like He doesn't care about us, especially when you hear turnaround testimonies of reconciliation and things you wish would happen for you but don't. This, of course, affects our relationship with God. I don't deconstruct my faith because, at my core, there's a strong belief I can't intellectually deny that God is present and that He is good. What's so confusing is that He just doesn't seem to be there for me and so, particularly when my daughter died, I was angry at God.

A Christian friend, unhelpfully, told me that wasn't allowed. They said it was sinful. I redirected my anger from God to them right away. It's not their fault, but it was hurtful because I was trying to find a safe space to explain how I felt to a fellow believer. Since then, I've come to understand that God is big enough to take our anger, disappointment and sadness. He knows anyway. It doesn't make sense for me to feel these things and outwardly pretend it's fine with those close to me.

Living with uncertainty

I grew up with a strong connection to the Jewish community, through my school and church, where I was introduced to some excellent Jewish authors from a young age. I learned that Jews seem to have fewer problems not knowing the answers to things. They're OK questioning God. There's a dialogue I feel they have with God where there's a sense that they know God knows, and they will ask God to explain Himself. But if He doesn't, they can accept it; it's just God.

I don't think Christians are good at living with such uncertainty. We want to give someone a scripture or spiritual discipline to fix things. We seem to think encouragement is giving the solution to the situation. From my experience of Jewish culture, they don't have that same solution-based approach. I believe a lot of discouragement comes from thinking that we're part of a solution-based belief system, but it doesn't work out. That's difficult. I don't like not knowing the answer to things. In life, I want to know what I should be doing, not doing and where I'm meant to be going. Life, unfortunately, is not like that. But openness to mystery can teach us that uncertainty isn't a lack of faith; it's an invitation to trust.

Try journalling

I've found journalling helpful in coping with the ambiguities of the Christian life. I'm a writer, and I like writing. When I read back what I've written, I find encouragement in how much I actually trusted God. I can see how I'd been holding on to Him. There've been times when I've not written much, if anything, because I've been distraught, but I can see that I kept coming back to God. This encourages me because it reveals something unbreakable between me and God. I encourage you to give it a try.

Finding affirming friends

It's also very helpful to have friends who affirm you when you don't feel like you can yourself. Yes, we talk a lot about self-care these days, which I agree with. But sometimes, we can't do that properly. We need others to speak into our lives positively, showing us what we've forgotten, like who we are in Christ and what He's done through us. Recently, a friend encouraged me by reminding me that I wrote the CV that got them their first job, which opened the door to a fruitful career. I'd completely forgotten. Their encouragement made me think, 'Oh, I can do this. I have done stuff, and I can do more.'

I think it's difficult not to be discouraged in our social media-saturated culture that promotes material prosperity and a church scene that prioritises spiritual 'success' stories. I've had to fight jealousy-inducing discouragement because I could see people on a similar trajectory to me doing better financially and in their relationships. We started at the same place, but they're getting the opportunities I'm not.

Wise friends are crucial to reminding us about what's important. I had someone close to me say, 'God isn't as interested in where you are at in life. He's most interested in what that means, what He's teaching you and where He's taking you.' That was hard to hear initially. But it's important because everyone's trajectory looks different, and that's for a reason. Mature Christians teach us that obedience to God doesn't necessarily result in material blessing from God. They can challenge us to pursue a more biblical approach to success.

Avoiding the comparison trap

One of the best ways to avoid the comparison trap I've found is to flee social media. Although we have a social media coordinator at work, I don't have my own personal accounts, which is probably to my detriment from a publishing point of view. I monitored my emotional wellbeing when I logged out of platforms, and it would be in the gutter; I found it was better to take myself off it completely.

If you don't leave Facebook, Instagram, Threads, TikTok or X feeling your happy self, I'd encourage you to limit your time on them or cut them out entirely, because they're not building you up. I'm not saying avoid things that make you feel uncomfortable, because that can sometimes help us grow. But if you're feeling low after you've engaged with them, that's something to pay attention to, because these habitual practices shape the person we are every day.

Taking one day at a time

I'm constantly unpacking what success really looks like. Part of me still seeks to serve cultural and parental ideals, even though I know in my core that educational and career achievements are not the primary markers of success. Although I still wrestle with this, what I try to do now, despite it sounding like a cliché, is to take one day at a time. It sounds obvious because what else can you do? But in this practice, I find peace – a sense of rest – because every day, I just think, 'Well, as long as I'm where God wants me to be, then I'm successful.' I don't know about tomorrow right now. I just know today, so I pray and ask for my daily bread for today. This helps me to focus on doing what

God wants me to do in the here and now, trusting and obeying Him. That seems like a successful place to me.

My default tendency can be busying myself to please people, so I need to remember that God isn't calling me to strive in that way. He's calling me to rest in Him. I'm learning that trusting God and calmly listening to Him in a posture of waiting is me being in His will. However, if your default is to hesitantly take a long time to do the things God is calling you to do, then trusting Him and being in His will may be to do the opposite. The way God works with each one of us is different.

Encouraging strangers

Loving my neighbours has also helped me. In a holy moment in a church service, God prompted me to hold a friend's child, something I hadn't done for a long time since losing Annie. It was so hard but also so healing. It released me later, at a coffee shop in London, where people typically don't talk to strangers, to obey God and encourage a pregnant woman (someone I previously might have felt bitter towards). It was just a simple prayer of blessing that I sensed she needed; there was no other exchange. She just looked grateful and said, 'Thank you.' But it helped my healing because I felt I was doing something good for God.

Learning scriptures

I don't know if you've ever asked God to give you a meaningful scripture verse. On one occasion, when I did that, Psalm 27:15 came into my head. Only it turns out it doesn't exist. Psalm 27 ends with verse 14. I was so confused. I thought, 'God, what is this?' and 'Is the devil putting random scriptures in my head?' Then I read verses 13-14 that would precede it:

> I remain confident of this:
> I will see the goodness of the LORD
> in the land of the living.
> Wait for the LORD;
> be strong and take heart
> and wait for the LORD.

I sensed God saying, 'That missing scripture is you, waiting. That's what I'm inviting you to do. You've read the scripture, now sit in it, in the waiting space between, hoping, being brave and courageous.' It so encouraged me. It reminded me that God has a warm sense of humour and gave me divine permission not to just do for Him but to be with Him and wait on Him.

It's really important to have scriptures that are pertinent to you specifically. Ask God for them and learn them so you can recite them whenever necessary. It's like the more you say them, the more they become part of you. John 10:10 is one of mine: 'The thief comes only to steal and kill and destroy; I have come that they may have life, and have it to the full.' It speaks to me because I like to enjoy life. I went out recently with a friend, and we laughed so much together that my ribs started aching. Laughter really is medicine for the soul. This sense of joyous abandon, however, is something we can lose as we get into adulthood, which is a shame since it's such a great antidote to discouragement.

Celebrating the small things

Another of my verses is Romans 8:28. Paul penned it in a context of persecution. Knowing this reminds us that its promise isn't about getting what we want, but about trusting God's redemptive work in every twist and turn of our journey. I particularly like it because when things go wrong, I can catastrophise quickly and snowball into 'life won't be worth living' thoughts. Romans 8:28 helps to break this cycle.

I recently had to move my belongings from the first floor of a large storage facility. But in the days before, the lift wasn't working. I started to worry, 'How am I going to do this?' Then Romans 8:28 came to mind, and I told myself, 'God's going to work this out for my good. I don't know how, but He will.' After a restless night's sleep holding on to this verse, I emailed the removers and asked, 'What's your plan for this situation?' They ended up enlisting extra people who carried everything down the stairs for me, and I moved to my new apartment in about half the allotted time.

It taught me that Romans 8:28 is less about the outcome of a specific promise and more about a promising outcome. It's not saying, 'They're going to fix the lift,' which would have been great. I would have wanted that. But actually, the outcome was way better. That's a small thing that happened. It didn't change any of the big things for me, but it helped me see God at work in the details of my daily life. It encouraged me to start being more grateful for the many good, small things God is doing. Zooming in on the small things I can be grateful for has really helped me stay encouraged while facing challenging big things, and I believe it will for you, too.

12

Is there enough grace in your gait?

Do you ever feel like you have to *earn* your place in life? Like every success has to be justified, every mistake paid for and every opportunity defended? It's an exhausting way to live. It's exactly the burden placed on Private James Ryan in the iconic film *Saving Private Ryan*.[81] It was the dying message Captain Miller whispered to Ryan. Ryan must guiltily work hard for the rest of his life. Hoping – somehow – he might justify the bloody sacrifice of Miller and the men sent to rescue him – never knowing whether what he's done is enough.

That is not a happy way to live. Thankfully, we don't have that ringing in our ears. The should-ery and ought-ery of such oppressive religiosity – ie, do this to be accepted by God – is like being frogmarched. It's not how Jesus desires us to walk with Him. He wants us to be compelled by His kindness; transformed by the unmerited favour bestowed upon each of us. It's a walk with a hop, skip and a jump – a joyful gait. God doesn't say, 'Earn it,' but, 'Honour me.' This shift changes everything. We're not

---

[81] 1998; distributed by DreamWorks Pictures; Paramount Pictures; FilmFlex.

living to prove our worth but to reflect His. Instead of constantly trying to measure up, we get to pour out – paying forward the grace we've already received. How? By letting our 'conversation be always full of grace' (Colossians 4:6), renouncing worldly ways and living 'godly lives' (Titus 2:11-14). And by offering grace to others, we enjoy it more ourselves!

It's hard, however, not to succumb to the temptation to live by a titillating love of legalism. Our cultural ambassadors, from celebrities to influencers, normalise the mantra, 'Earn before you deserve.'[82] Without even noticing, we can find ourselves slipping into the restrictive straitjacket of ungrace, where striving overtakes thriving. And dare I write that sometimes, at least initially, it can fit a little too comfortably? By this, I mean justify-your-existence legalism can have the 'appearance of wisdom' to us and others (Colossians 2:23). We can see it in the labelling of people as 'deserving' or 'underserving' of our help. It's the voice that says, 'They should have worked harder,' or, 'They brought it on themselves.' We might not say it out loud, but if we're honest, many of us have thought it. Perhaps it's a proud desire to boost our self-esteem by looking down on others.

---

[82] '"Earn before you deserve": Matthew McConaughey shares wisdom with followers', *The Independent*, www.independent.co.uk/tv/lifestyle/matthew-mcconaughey-hollywood-advice-fans-b2136357.html (accessed 3rd January 2025).

Pause!

Where might you have succumbed to seeking to earn your place, in life and with God?

We will not share with them

This spirit of ungrace got hold of some of David's soldiers. Picture it: David and his men have just returned from battle, tired but with arms full of loot. But as soon as they saw the 200 blokes who stayed behind, some of the victorious troops resentfully grumbled, 'Because they did not go out with us, we will not share with them the plunder we recovered' (1 Samuel 30:22). Its logic makes sense in this world of earning our keep – but David saw it differently.

Instead of dividing the spoils based on effort, David declared, 'All shall share alike' (1 Samuel 30:24). Sound familiar? It's the same approach Jesus took in the parable of the vineyard workers in Matthew 20:1-16. Everyone, from the early birds to the latecomers, got the same pay. It's the kind of grace that makes people uncomfortable – and that's precisely the point. David knew neither he nor they deserved this victory. It was underserved blessing from God. It would therefore have been unjust for them not to extend the same generosity to others.

Showing grace to others is a sign we're still savouring it ourselves. When we become stingy, mean-spirited and belligerent about our rights, we've often forgotten the undeserved riches of the 'great love the Father has lavished on us' (1 John 3:1). It's easy, for example, to look down on the unmerciful servant from Jesus' parable in Matthew 18:21-35. He was forgiven a massive debt but refused to pay it forward to someone who owed him only a few pounds. If we're honest, we may be more like him than we'd like to admit. Ever forgiven someone, only to resent them later when they messed up again? Guilty? Me too; that's the unmerciful servant in us. However, when we remember how much we've been forgiven by God, we become more generous with our words and actions.

As our time together begins to draw to a close, I want to leave you with a powerful practice that's easy to overlook when discouragement creeps in.

Worship

Almost everyone I spoke with shared how worship songs help them hold on to hope. It's not surprising, since worship helps us remember and revel in the grace of God. Worship – trumpet blasts and shouts – helped to break down the walls of Jericho in Joshua 6. Worship brought relief to an oppressed king in 1 Samuel 16:23. Worship cut through chains and opened doors for Paul and Silas in prison in Acts 16:25-26.

The song that helped me out of the grave of discouragement was 'I Thank God' by Maverick City Music. Have a listen and I think you'll understand why.[83]

Hea Woo spent several years in a North Korean prison. She faced mental and physical torture. But in that place, she planted a tiny church. They met in the only place the guards wouldn't go – the disgusting toilets. There, they whisper-worshipped 'Amazing Grace' to avoid being

---

[83] www.youtube.com/watch?v=LM1qrx0Huds (accessed 7th February 2024).

overheard. Looking back on that time, Hea Woo said: 'Worship and praise is the antidote to discouragement.'[84]

Stop and think

- What is grace, and how have you experienced it in your life?

- Is there someone you could offer grace to today – who doesn't deserve it – because you've already generously received it from God?

- What worship song(s) could you soak in?

[84] Open Doors UK & Ireland, *Secret Church Resource*, Leaders Guide, media.opendoorsuk.org/document/pdf/2023-Secret%20Church-update.pdf (accessed 24th January 2025), p 5.

13
Forgive freely
Dr R T Kendall

Robert Tillman (R T) Kendall served as the senior minister at Westminster Chapel, London, for twenty-five years. Widely recognised as one of the most influential Christian leaders and teachers in both the United States and the United Kingdom, he has authored numerous books and remains in high demand as a speaker around the globe. For more information, visit rtkendallministries.com

Losing heart

Discouragement is when we lose heart, feel like we can't continue and have nothing to live for. I would violate my preaching on total forgiveness if I shared the details of my hurts and hardships. The temptation to share does come from time to time – you want everybody to know – but total forgiveness, as I've taught before, includes protecting those who've wronged you by not exposing them. It means releasing them entirely into God's hands, and I seek to live by that. All I can say is that when I was at Westminster Chapel, things occurred that were unfair and unjust, and I couldn't tell anybody. It was the worst moment of my life.

I was deeply discouraged; it looked like the future was so bleak and that I was finished. Only, I was blessed.

The hidden power of forgiveness

God sent an old friend into my life, and I decided to tell him what had happened because I knew he wouldn't tell anybody. I thought he would probably put his arm around me and say, 'R T, get it out of your system; you ought to be angry.' I wanted him to justify my hurt. He just said, 'Anything more?'

I said, 'No, that's it.'

Then he said, 'You must totally forgive them. Until you totally forgive them, you will be in chains. Release them, and you will be released.'

Nobody had ever talked to me like that. It was both the hardest and the kindest word anybody ever gave me.

I can look at you now and say, under a lie detector, that the worst moment in my life has turned out to be the best. It was very wrong. I don't justify them at all. I'm just grateful. God used that to get my attention, and He got my attention. I never dreamed I'd write a book on it one day.

The way I got out of that discouraging season was forgiveness. I knew I'd made that breakthrough when I could pray for them, ask God to bless them and know I meant it. But as recently as a month ago, I reached another level. I didn't think there would be another one. Let me explain what I mean. But first, why am I talking about forgiveness? Because discouragement often feeds on hidden bitterness, which can fuel burnout. Recognising this chain can help us break free at its weakest link: unforgiveness.

Greater depths of forgiveness

In 1 Corinthians 4:3, Paul, having been accused by the Corinthians, responded, 'I care very little if I am judged by you or by any human court; indeed, I do not even judge myself.' But he added, 'Wait until the Lord comes. He will bring to light what is hidden in darkness' (v 5). In other words, leave it to God, and it will all come out at the judgement. This is what kept me going: one day, everybody will know. But now, are you ready for this? I don't say we've got to do this, but I am saying we need it. I'm saying this is what I had to do as recently as a month ago.

I was looking at that verse in the context of Stephen being stoned to death in Acts 7. His last words were not, 'God will get them for this.' They were not, 'Wait till the judgement day; you're going to be in big trouble.' Do you know what he said? 'Lord, do not hold this sin against them' (Acts 7:60). He didn't even want them judged on the final day! That challenged me: I realised I hadn't extended that level of mercy yet. I've kept my principles, such as, don't tell what they did. But while I was practising that, I still thought, 'Oh, one day the truth will be out,' and I wanted to see the look on their faces when they were exposed.

Only, all my life, I've wanted the anointing; that's what Stephen had. So, a month ago, I said, 'Lord, I pray for these that they won't even get caught or found out at the judgement.' I meant it, and I'll tell you something: the peace I got was so wonderful. Now I've got a new level of total forgiveness that I don't think I've ever talked about publicly. The bitterness goes when you totally forgive. It eases burnout and detoxes discouragement. Stephen was anointed. God was able to trust him with His powerful presence. I mean, look at his knowledge of the Bible. Look at the vision he had: seeing Jesus standing at the right hand of God. What's more, Stephen's face was shining like an angel. What's the explanation? That he went to a university? That he prayed more? No, I think it comes down to forgiveness; he prayed they wouldn't even get caught.

You might try this yourself: write down the names of those who've hurt you and pray, 'Lord, don't let them suffer for what they did to me. Free them from judgement – forever.' It's challenging, but as you release them, you'll find yourself released as well.

Learning to please God above all

My life verse is John 5:44. It's about glorifying God and not getting approval from others. In 1956, when I was twenty-one years old, this verse came into my mind. I decided I wouldn't live by what other people would think of me. Instead, I've made it my practice to ask God what He would like. It doesn't mean I don't like other people's praise; it's just that that's not what I'm living for. It's not easy, not least because we often want God to please us. It's like me praying, 'Lord, You'd make me very happy today if You fulfilled those prophecies about revival.' But that would be Him pleasing me. What if God gets more glory by making me wait a little longer? We need to get our encouragement from knowing we're pleasing God because we're aligned with His good and perfect timings, not our own. We must find out what pleases God and do that, and learn what grieves the Holy Spirit and not do that.[85]

---

[85] Ephesians 4:29-32 is a good place to start and keep coming back to.

Feeling what others are going through

Jesus didn't rebuke or say, 'Shame on you,' to the discouraged. When Mary and Martha blamed Him for not stopping Lazarus from dying, and Mary was crying her heart out, what was Jesus' response? The shortest verse in the Bible, John 11:35: 'Jesus wept.' He just felt what she felt. He could have said, 'Shh, be quiet. I will raise him from the dead in a minute if you just be quiet.' No, He wept. He entered into their pain. He covered them. That's what we must do for each other in discouragement. We must try to feel what others are going through, empathise with them and encourage them not to give up.

14
Where are you?

We've covered a good deal of ground in this book: exploring deep questions and, hopefully, experiencing glimpses of God's heart and healing presence. Now, before we move on to the concluding chapter and draw everything together, let's pause and reflect on our journey with God's first question – the father of them all.

It's also our seventh, and so it's a sort of sabbatical question, inviting us to rest in the light and easy yoke of Christ.[86] As mentioned in the Introduction, it calls us out of hiding to bask in God's nurturing presence and confront life's challenging realities with the strength bestowed by heaven.

This deliberately brief chapter allows us space to spend more quality time in thoughtful reflection with the One who asks, 'Where are you?' – not to shame us but to assure us that we are seen, heard and wonderfully loved.

---

[86] Matthew 11:30.

Stop and think

- *Where are you with God?* Consider your walk with Him over the course of these chapters. Have you noticed any shifts in how you relate to Him or hear His voice?

- *Where are you with yourself?* Pause to notice your own heart. Are there areas that have softened or places that still seem guarded?

- *Where are you with others?* Reflect on how your relationships have been influenced by what you've read. Are you engaging with people – friends, family, colleagues and neighbours – differently?

- *Where are you?* Finally, come back to this question in its purest form. Trust again that God wants to meet you in this moment, no matter how you feel. He already knows where you are, but longs to hear you articulate it as you invite Him into every hidden corner of your life. Receive any insight, conviction or joy that surfaces as you linger with this question in prayer.

15
Conclusion

The Lord's Prayer – Matthew 6:9-13 and Luke 11:2-4 – can be used to summarise the journey we've been on together.

Our Father

God is not a stingy Ebenezer Scrooge caricature. He's 'the Father [source and reservoir] of compassion and the God of all comfort' (2 Corinthians 1:3). Seeing Him rightly – His merciful generosity – shuts down discouragement, so we must begin this way. As no doubt you know, Jesus used radical, intimate, personal language here for His contemporary Jewish listeners, inviting them to call the Lord, 'Father'. We are crawling into the lap of the best dad imaginable as we prayerfully bring the state of our souls to Him.

in heaven

Heaven is a place of sinless glory, where God is sovereignly reigning; that's where our *hope* resides. But it isn't just transcendent (above). It's also imminent (near). 'Heaven' could also be translated as 'air'. Meaning: every location and place at the same time. 'Our Father is always near us' is how Professor Dallas Willard put it.[87]

Hallowed be

Here, we rightly *remember* the awesome One we're privileged to pray to as we declare truths about His character. It's about seeing God as He is, resplendent in glorious goodness, savouring Him and then seeking Him based on His excellent nature.

Your kingdom

Prayer is an act of surrender. It's about 'Your', not 'my'. It says, 'God, Your way is the best way. What You want, I want.' It's *enquiring* of the Lord, asking for His good, pleasing and perfect rule to grow in our hearts and increasingly come through His Church.

Give us

Now, we start to pray for our needs (not greeds). Bread is an essential, not a luxury. It speaks of both spiritual and material necessities. God's Word is our daily bread,[88] but we also need food, water, shelter, relationships and all the human essentials we can think of. These verses also challenge us to live one day at a time: not overwhelming ourselves with worries about the future, but focusing on being trustfully present in the current twenty-four hours.

---

[87] Dallas Willard, *The Divine Conspiracy: Rediscovering Our Hidden Life in God*, New York: HarperCollins e-books, 2014, p 372.
[88] Matthew 4:4.

The language in this skeleton prayer is *'Our* Father', not 'My Father'; *'Your* will', not 'my will'; 'give *us'*, not 'give me'. We're no longer competing against each other but are in authentic community with one another, praying for each other's (and our *neighbours')* needs – and being the answer to those prayers in an Acts 2:44-45 and 4:32-37 way.

Forgive

This part of the prayer allows us to search our hearts and let God shine His gentle spotlight on any 'offensive way' within us that we should confess (Psalm 139:24). It's sincere sorrow over any wrong done and a cry to experience the forgiveness Jesus has won.

To fully enjoy forgiveness, however, we must also offer it. Discouragement and resentment are intriguingly intertwined. So often, we rehearse and even cherish hurtful things said or spoken over us. We can let the devil live rent-free in our heads, encouraged by him to bitterly wallow in what has wounded us.

But we will not find freedom until we forgive and stop giving the lies the life they need to persist. Holding on to unforgiveness for wrongs done to us grieves God. As has been said, unforgiveness is drinking yourself the poison you intended for the other person.[89] The antidote is forgiveness. It's choosing not to bring to remembrance. It's facing the pain and letting go. It's agreeing to live with the consequences of another person's sin.

---

[89] This saying is often attributed to American author Marianne Williamson, as well as others. See www.brainyquote.com/quot es/marianne_williamson_635346 (accessed 7th February 2025).

Deliver

This closing part of the prayer is a call to remember that the Christian life isn't *like* a war; it *is* a war! We should again recognise there are real reasons why our inner self may be melting away – three of them: the world, the flesh and the devil. We must, therefore, be praying for protection, and not just for ourselves. We should ask for strength to resist how they work together to demoralise and discourage. It's a prayer for watchfulness, alertness and total victory against evil.

Yours is

This later addition by the Church reminds us to respond rightly to God. It's an opportunity for us to choose again to reside in God's kingdom, power and glory. And not to hide, like Adam and Eve, in our fig-leaf-like, inadequate and discouraging versions of them. We embrace God's will and reject self-rule. We abide in His mighty resurrection power (that's made perfect in our weakness).[90] And we long for the whole earth to be filled with the outshining of His glorious character. We resolve to live in His kingdom, live by His power and live for His glory.

If you're wondering how we can put into practice the material we've been working through together, start with the Lord's Prayer. Read each line, then say or write out a corresponding prayer in your own words. I pray that as you say it often, the peaceful presence of God will detoxify

---

[90] 2 Corinthians 12:9.

your discouragement. May you ever increasingly know the encouragement of the Lord.

Kintsugi Hope
Journeying towards wholeness

Kintsugi Hope is a Christian mental health charity dedicated to creating safe, supportive spaces where people can explore their mental and emotional wellbeing. Its mission is inspired by the Japanese art of *kintsugi* – the practice of repairing broken pottery with gold, transforming cracks into something beautiful. In the same way, Kintsugi Hope believes our emotional, physical and spiritual scars are not signs of failure but reflections of strength, resilience and hope.

At the core of Kintsugi Hope's work is a deep commitment to restore hope and wholeness for those navigating mental health challenges, loneliness and societal pressures. It offers a range of resources and programmes designed to equip individuals, churches and communities with the tools to address mental health in a way that integrates faith, compassion and practical support.

How you can get involved

There are many ways to become part of Kintsugi Hope's mission to bring health and wholeness to communities:

- *Join a Wellbeing Group*: Participate in a local, safe, non-judgemental space where you can be honest about your mental health, connect with others and walk together towards wholeness.

- *Train as a group leader*: Take an active role in your community by becoming a trained Kintsugi Hope facilitator.

- *Attend a training event or workshop*: Kintsugi Hope offers training for churches on how to better support those navigating mental health challenges.

- *Give or donate*: Support the ongoing work of Kintsugi Hope by making a donation. Every contribution, large or small, helps fund Wellbeing Groups, facilitator training and the creation of new mental health resources.

I used to feel like I had to hide my struggles with anxiety and depression. But joining a Kintsugi Hope Wellbeing Group changed everything. I realised I wasn't alone, and my story wasn't something to be ashamed of. The group gave me space to be vulnerable, to listen to others and to be truly seen. I'm even training to become a facilitator so I can help others find that same freedom.

Sarah, Kintsugi Hope participant

To learn more about Kintsugi Hope's life-changing work, visit www.kintsugihope.com

Open Doors UK & Ireland
Standing with the persecuted Church

Around the world, more than 380 million Christians face persecution simply for their faith. They endure harassment, discrimination, imprisonment and even violence. Open Doors UK & Ireland is part of a global ministry dedicated to serving persecuted Christians in more than seventy countries. For seventy years, Open Doors has worked to strengthen the global Church by providing practical support, spiritual resources and advocacy. This includes delivering Bibles to underground churches, offering trauma care to those affected by persecution and helping displaced Christians rebuild their lives.

Persecution is not just a distant issue – it is a call to action for Christians everywhere. The Bible reminds us in Hebrews 13:3: 'Continue to remember those in prison as if you were together with them in prison, and those who are ill-treated as if you yourselves were suffering.' By supporting Open Doors, you stand in solidarity with the persecuted Church, reminding them they are not alone.

Getting involved with Open Doors UK & Ireland is simple but impactful. Here's how:

- *Pray*: Join the global prayer movement for persecuted Christians. Open Doors offers prayer guides and updates to focus your intercession.

- *Give*: Your donations provide essential support, from food and shelter for displaced believers to training for church leaders in hostile areas.

- *Advocate*: Raise your voice for those who cannot speak for themselves. Sign petitions, write to your MP and participate in Open Doors' campaigns to influence change.

- *Raise awareness*: Host events in your church, share Open Doors' stories on social media or lead a small group study on persecution.

- *Stay connected*: Subscribe to Open Doors UK & Ireland's newsletter to stay informed about the latest news, prayer requests and opportunities to help.

When you partner with Open Doors, you become part of a global mission to 'strengthen what remains' (Revelation 3:2). Together, we can bring light to the shadows and stand firm with our persecuted family. Your journey starts here. Visit opendoorsuk.org to learn more, donate and join the movement today. Let's make a difference that echoes into eternity.

Acknowledgements

Thank You so much, God, for not giving up on me and gifting me the time to write this book and be encouraged by others. Thank you loads Holly, Anna and Isaac, for encouraging me and giving me so much joy. Thank you big-time, family and friends, for coming around us with unconditional love. Thank you, amazing contributors; your words gave me life when it felt like I was on life support. Thank you, Cathy Madavan, for your kind foreword, and everyone who endorsed the book; your support is a true blessing. Thank you to Lee at christianbookediting.co.uk and Amos at christianbookeditor.uk for helping a dyslexic author get the early manuscript up to scratch for submission to a publisher. Thank you to Instant Apostle for your faith in this project, wise counsel and impressive support throughout the publishing journey. Thank you to my Kintsugi Hope, Open Doors and Hope Church Ipswich families; it's a joy to serve alongside you. And thank you, dear reader. Please help to spread the word.